DOCTORS OF MODERNITY:

DARWIN
MARX
&
FREUD

DOCTORS OF MODERNITY:
DARWIN
MARX
&
FREUD

R. F. Baum

Sherwood Sugden & Company
PUBLISHERS

315 Fifth Street, Peru, Illinois 61354

First printing 1988.

Sherwood Sugden & Company, Publishers
315 Fifth Street
Peru, Illinois 61354

Library of Congress Cataloging-in-Publication Data

Baum, R. F.
    Doctors of modernity.

    Includes index.
    1. Darwin, Charles, 1809–1882. 2. Marx, Karl,
1818–1883. 3. Freud, Sigmund, 1856–1939. 4. Evolution.
5. Historical materialism. 6. Psychoanalysis. I. Title.
B1623.B34 1988   190   88-26456
ISBN 0-89385-215-5

TABLE OF CONTENTS

Of all errors, the most indecent attack our heritage of mind.

—Thomas Aquinas
De Anima

Our reason may be a pitiful candlelight in the dark and boundless seas of being. But we have nothing better, and woe to those who wilfully try to put it out.

—Morris Cohen
Reason and Nature

Introduction

For over a century Darwin, for nearly a century Marx and Freud, have exerted on the modern world an influence comparable to that exerted on medieval Europe by the Doctors of the Church. Nearly everywhere we look, whether to art and literature, manners and morals, psychosocial thought or political practice, we find 20th-century people thinking and acting in ways that manifest an ingestion, often quite unwitting, of the ideas of Darwin, Marx, and Freud. As Augustine, Ambrose, and their peers put a religious stamp on medieval civilization, so Darwin, Marx, and Freud have stamped with irreligion or, as many call it, humanism nearly every facet of modernity. Perceived as champions of untrammelled mind or reason, these three writers are also, or thereby, perceived as foes of every sort of obscurantism and of the social evils attributed to it. Although not modernity's founders, who must be looked for centuries earlier, Darwin, Marx, and Freud have become modernity's Doctors.

Darwinians may at once object to coupling Darwin with Marx and Freud. Darwin, they may feel, dealt in science, while Marx and Freud fathered para-religious faiths. But there is little doubt that Darwin created a ready audience for Marx and Freud, and there is no doubt at all that Marxists and Freudians acclaim and honor Darwin. The difference pointed to may to some extent exist, but in the following pages we shall find it smaller than Darwinians often think.

There have, of course, and from the first, been rumblings of discontent with the high status conferred upon each of these three writers. Today perhaps more than ever certain Darwinian, Marxian, and Freudian propositions encounter both learned and popular dissent. No biologist acquainted with genetics seems likely to attribute to natural selection the creative, as distinguished from pruning, power that Darwin initially claimed for it. No one, and probably least of all the peoples of Russia and eastern Europe, expects Marxist revolution to inaugurate a classless society. Freud's more bizarre reflections on sexuality occasion mainly laughter in college dormitories male and female or, as thanks in part to Freud dormitories sometimes are, combined. Yet deep respect, amounting to veneration, still hallows the names of Darwin, Marx, and Freud. Challenged, it grows belligerent.

Publicly to describe Darwinian evolution theory as in truth a *theory* and not a proven fact invites, as Ronald Reagan discovered while campaigning for the presidency, description of oneself as scientifically illiterate. Not to agree with the Harvard sociologist Daniel Bell that in discussion of society "the starting point, necessarily, is Marx" imperils social scientists' chances of academic promotion. Openly to describe psychoanalysis as grotesque and uncontrolled speculation suffices to mark one out as unimaginative and hidebound. Although specific statements gained our Doctors their renown, the respect paid them today transcends specifics. Its object is not only and often not mainly anything specific but instead an "approach" or "insight" that functions as a fundamental principle.

Meanwhile the imposing theoretical constructions in which our Doctors articulated that usually unstated principle are known only vaguely and in disjointed fragments to most of the educated public. The same public seem largely unaware that radical and unanswered objections to those constructions have been put forward by specialists eminent in our Doctors' respective fields and by philosophers as weighty as Karl Popper, P. A. Sorokin, Morris Cohen, Michael Polanyi, and Eric Voegelin.

This short book means concisely to present the theories with which Darwin, Marx, and Freud engraved their signatures on nearly all modernity. The book goes on to risk the wrath of conventional opinion by, instead of searching the same theories for hidden wisdom, subjecting them to empirical and logical test. In consequence, it arrives at quite a different view of them from the one conventionally accepted. It finds that instead of championing human mind or reason Darwin, Marx, and Freud set in train a dangerous derogation of it.

Consider:

From Darwin stems the idea that competitive brute struggle for existence produced and in the last analysis still governs all existing species, including man. From Marx stems the idea that economic need and interest determine human thought and history. To Freud we owe the notion that human beings are driven and in the end accounted for by a mainly sexual "libido."

Those conceptions have been acclaimed as healthy correctives of Victorian prudishness or of undue confidence in human rationality. Unfortunately, taken singly or together, they nourish the suspicion or plant the firm conviction that man's mind, in which Jews and Christians found the image of a free Creator, acts merely as the pliant, rationalizing agent of sub-rational drives.

No doubt unintentionally, but nonetheless in fact, Darwin, Marx, and Freud have gone far toward persuading educated people that opinions and ideas do little more than register the instincts and the circumstances of those who hold them. Hence all ideas come to seem equally involuntary and irrational, hence equally true or false—or, as many have learned to write and think it, equally "true" or "false" in sophisticated quotes. Where that suspicion or conviction gains a lodging, any effort toward impersonal or objective truth seems naive; any claim to base belief on fact and logic becomes the object of a knowing smile.

Such sophistication teeters on the edge of nihilism, and frequently falls in. It is dangerous because it tends at every point of human disagreement to denigrate and preclude rational argument. If unchecked, it will make force, perhaps at first the force of money or World Opinion but ultimately the force of numbers and weapons not the last but the first resort. However unwitting and unintentional on our Doctors' part, the very faculties and discipline required to prevent an always-easy slide into brutishness are discouraged, undermined, belittled. It does not seem an accident that a century aiming confidently at Progress and applying to Darwin, Marx, and Freud for marching orders has been a century of world wars, genocide, and totalitarian tyrannies.

That a doctrine is unwelcome or demoralizing does not necessarily prove it false. Reflective people will, however, want to scrutinize it with some care. To say that human intellect may err is healthy. To declare it finally in bondage to circumstance and instinct is not. It seems safe to say that as long as Darwin, Marx, and Freud remain our Doctors, the political and moral disasters of this century will continue. To no small extent the hope of non-violent resolution of the differences that beset our increasingly precarious civilization depends on quashing the derogations of man's mind inherent in the doctrines examined in the following pages. At stake is a conception loaded with more meaning for the future than any that computers, cyclotrons, or telescopes can provide. At stake is our conception of ourselves and of our fellow men.

No reader taking up a book as short as this will expect it to examine everything advanced by writers as prolific as the three we shall consider. Still less will he expect coverage of the enormous mass of commentary they have inspired. Concerned with the doctrines that gained our Doctors the world's attention, this book focusses on those doctrines and ignores peripheral reflections. It finds that those doctrines undercut and nullify their own claims to rationality and that they stand at odds with sometimes obvious fact. It also brings to light what few educators have told their students, what few commentators have told the reading public, that insuperable objections to the same doctrines occasioned large, even comprehensive, withdrawals of them by Darwin, Marx, and Freud themselves.

The book's Conclusion considers and seeks to account for what can be called soft or sophisticated Darwinism, Marxism, and Freudianism. These are positions taken by educators and other intellectuals who acknowledge many of our Doctors' crucial errors but who still pay them ardent homage. Here the approach or insight mentioned earlier, one that functions as a fundamental principle, becomes the issue. The Conclusion identifies it as philosophical naturalism, in plain words atheism, and points out that it accounts for what is baneful in our Doctors' teaching. The conclusion also emphasizes that what is sound and convincing in the same teaching harmonizes easily with, and indeed restates, authentic Judeo-Christian wisdom.

Chapter I
Darwinism

A notable fact has been overlooked: to this day those best qualifed to render a clear verdict on the truth or falsity of Darwinian evolution theory have not rendered it. Nearly all biologists accept evolution itself or, as Darwin called it, descent with modification as a valid inference from geology and the fossil record. But Darwinism claims more. Darwinism claims that evolution is caused and explained by *natural selection*. That is Darwinism, and it aroused so many objections from Darwin's fellow naturalists that Darwin devoted the greater part of *The Origin of Species* as we read that book today, in the last of his many revisions, to attempts to answer them.

Among modern biologists professed Darwinians easily outnumber non-Darwinians, but the ranks of the latter are growing. A generation ago biologists as eminent as Richard Goldschmidt and Lecomte du Noüy advanced radical objections to selection theory, and their objections have not been successfully answered. Today paleontologists and molecular biologists are seeking non-Darwinian explanations of evolution. Today also, even professed Darwinians freely admit facts impossible to square with Darwin's conception of evolution as, thanks to natural selection, a process inherently progressive and indefinitely continuing.

The objections and admissions noted raise a question not easily disposed of: might Darwin's theory of evolution have owed its popular success less to its scientific value than because it projected into biology, or stated in biological terms, a popular philosophy or worldview?

When *Origin of Species* came from the press in 1859 both philosophical naturalism and its surrogate for religious hope, the idea of Progress, were in ascendance. Few people objected when the physicist Laplace declared God an "unnecessary hypothesis." Moreover, as had occurred long before in Greece and Rome, the idea of Progress and the idea of the development of existing forms of life from simpler forms of the past had appeared together.[1] Toward the end of the 17th century the philosopher Leibniz had announced a "perfecting principle" that in his view operated throughout the universe and in its forms of life. In the 18th century the French naturalist Buffon had contended against the notion of species' immutability, and Progressist thinkers like Diderot and Rousseau had plumped specifically for biological progress. By the start of the 19th century the idea of progressive evolution had gained sufficient currency for Darwin's grandfather, Erasmus Darwin, to put it into didactic verse. In 1844 Robert Chambers, a British publisher, had laid out a detailed scheme of evolutionary progress in *The Vestiges of the Natural History of Creation*. Conversely, at the same period the poet Coleridge had warmly rejected "the Oran-Utang theory of the origin of the human race."

All these men, and subsequently Charles Darwin, conceived evolution as a continuing process producing ever higher forms of life. As such it accorded perfectly with the Progress idea adumbrated by Leibniz and triumphant,

---

* Publisher's note: In this book I have introduced a little wrinkle that I hope, by proving useful to the reader, will one day become a standard convention: note flags which are references only are set in italic type; those of substance are signalled by being set in bold.

before Darwin, in the philosophies of Condorcet, Hegel, Comte, and Spencer. By giving progress a foundation in biology, by making human history an extension or a function of a vastly longer, progressive biological process, evolution as Darwin came to present and explain it, powerfully recommended itself to his contemporaries on philosophical grounds.

To judge the significance of that statement we should remember that in Darwin's day the empirical, fossil evidence for evolution, though recognized as such, was scanty and that after his own efforts to augment that evidence Darwin acknowledged it open to serious objection. Yet in a letter to Darwin his onetime teacher, the geologist Adam Sedgwick, was able to write, "We all admit [biological] development as a fact of history: but how came it about?"[2] Among scientists a climate of opinion strongly naturalistic and Progressist had very nearly settled on evolution as an historical fact. The question agitating scientists was much less if, than *how*, evolution occurred. A generation earlier the French evolutionist Lamarck had tried to answer that question with the notion that new traits acquired by individuals in their lifetimes were inherited by their offspring. Ordinary observation refuted that—people who had greatly strengthened their mental or physical abilities frequently had mediocre children—and left the question unanswered.

Among scientists the great age of the earth, the nature of fossils, and the struggle for existence had all been recognized. So had the eliminative pruning action of natural selection. In the Historical Sketch that Darwin prefixed to a late edition of the *Origin* he acknowledged not only his predecessor evolutionists but also the recognition of natural selection by several of them. He wrote, for example, that a paper read before the Royal Society in 1813 by William

Charles Wells "distinctly recognizes the principle of natural selection." In 1834 Sir Charles Lyell in his *Principles of Geology* had written, "In the universal struggle for existence the right of the strongest eventually prevails."[3] In the 11th (1877) edition of the same classic work Lyell wrote:

> In former editions of this work from 1832 to 1853, I did not venture to differ from the opinions of Linnaeus, that each species had remained from its origin as we now see it, being variable, but only within certain fixed limits . . . . [But] I pointed out how the struggle for existence among species, and the increase and spread of some of them, must tend to the extermination of others.[4]

Hence, though evolution itself is widely coupled with Darwin's name and conceived as he conceived it, he originated neither that idea nor the idea of natural selection. With Alfred Russell Wallace, Darwin contributed instead the idea that natural selection *caused* evolution. "The Origin of Species By Means of Natural Selection," as Darwin phrased his idea in his book's title, was his actual contribution. By seeming to answer the question "How?" it appeared to clinch the question of evolution itself; and by answering the question "How?" in the particular way it did it seemed to vindicate both Progressism and philosophical naturalism.

That philosophical naturalism requires some vindication will come home to anyone who reflects on its basic contention that natural or spatio-temporal phenomena constitute the whole of reality and that man and nature can in principle be explained without recourse to anything beyond them. As we shall see Marx admitting with regard to man in the following chapter, normal intelligence cannot help asking about man's origin or cause, presumably something different from man on which man depends for his existence. Here Marx satisfied himself, at least, by peremptorily declaring man self-created. Equally solicitous of naturalism, Auguste Comte had earlier advised abandoning the search for origins of anything. With *The Origin of Species* Darwin offered something more persuasive. Though not addressing the question of the origin or cause of nature, he appeared squarely to meet the question of animal, and by implication, human origin and to provide a thoroughly naturalistic answer. He did so with a theory seemingly so commonsensical and even obvious—"how very stupid not to have thought of it!" T. H. Huxley reproached himself—that the disquieting question seemed finally put to rest.

Impressed by a consideration emphasized earlier by Thomas Malthus, that animals tended to multiply faster than their food supply, Darwin reasoned that in the consequent struggle for existence those individuals who were blessed with "infinitesimally small" but biologically useful variations from their species' norms would be most likely to survive and reproduce. From this it seemed to him to follow that useful variations would accumulate, develop further over successive generations, and gradually result in new and biologically superior species.[5] In his Conclusion Darwin accordingly wrote that owing to natural selection "all corporeal and mental endowments will tend to progress towards perfection." "Thus," he concluded, "from the war of nature, from famine and death, the most exalted object which we are capable of conceiving, the production of the higher animals, directly follows. There is grandeur in this view of life . . . ."[6]

It was a view that appealed to a rising middle class by making Progress, seen by thinkers of the 18th century as a goal to be achieved by reason and good will, the normal and natural outcome of the play of ordinary tradesman instinct. Whatever succeeded or paid off would do so through an ultimately benign natural selection and therefore rightly should succeed and pay off. . . . For different reasons Darwin's view also appealed to Marx and other socialists. It appealed to them by implying species' unlimited malleability under the influence of environment. Marxists expected a remolded and improved society to remold and improve human nature, and to this Darwinism brought strong support.

For still other reasons Darwin's view of life appealed to certain factory owners and militarists, who made it the basis of the pitiless social philosophy called Social Darwinism.[7] Understandably, and to their credit opposed to Social Darwinism, present-day Darwinians declare that philosophy a "misuse" of Darwin's teaching. In fact, though, Social Darwinism seems no more a misuse of Darwin's teaching than Hitler's Final Solution seems a misuse of Hitler's teaching. Darwin's theory unquestionably meant that man owed his origin and human estate to favored individuals' success in a universal war of nature, at bottom to exercise of animal cunning and brute force. As Social Darwinists perceived, the theory also meant that favored individuals could and even should improve the human species by exploiting competitive advantage wherever that occurred. Only thus could they and their offspring assure further development of their allegedly superior traits. It was this exaltation of competition, of the "war of nature" and the faculties suited to it, that put Darwin into real and lasting conflict with religion. As his "bulldog" T. H. Huxley regretfully phrased the matter in his Romanes Lecture, good or virtuous conduct was "opposed to that which leads to success in the cosmic struggle for existence."[8]

As we all know, Darwin's theory conflicted also with the "creationist" notion that existing species are those originally created by God. As Darwin later wrote in *The Descent of Man*, to overcome that notion was one of his two aims in writing the *Origin*, the other being to establish natural selection as the cause of evolutionary change. But in fact, in repudiating the special-creation notion, Darwin was unwittingly following in the footsteps of no less a theologian than Augustine.

In writing about creation Augustine, whose authority throughout the Middle Ages ranked second only to the Gospels', wrote that the words "In the beginning God made the heavens and the earth" meant that God had made them and everything in them as the trunk, branches, and foliage of a tree are made in its seed, out of which, over time, they grow. According to Augustine, who warned that the six days of the Genesis creation story were not days as ordinarily spoken of by men, and whose account of Creation was later cited approvingly by Thomas Aquinas, God originally created not the world that men saw around them, but a world that, over time, would produce the world that men saw, a conception in complete accord with descent with modification or evolution. The "creationist" notion of the special creation and fixity of species has neither patristic nor medieval authority. It seems to have made its way into Catholic thought via the 17th-century Jesuit, Suarez, and into Protestant thought via Calvinist reverence for the letter of Scripture and Milton's literalist portrayal of Creation in *Paradise Lost*. In Darwin's day T. H. Huxley referred to it as "the Miltonic hypothesis."[9]

The basic idea that over time forms of life change into or produce spectacularly different forms carries no religious or moral implications. Darwin may have had that truth in mind when he wrote in his Conclusion, "I see no good reason why the views given in this volume should shock the religious feelings of anyone." What Darwin at that point did not perceive was that a religious and moral problem does most definitely arise if existing forms of life, including man, owe their being, as he said they did, to victory in a merciless war of nature. In Darwin's view, new species resulted from an accumulation of variations useful in a competitive struggle for food and self-reproduction. It was that conception of evolution's "how" or method, not his assertion of evolution itself, that brought him into real and fundamental conflict with religion. We can credit Darwin and Darwinism with discountenancing the literalist reading of Genesis and Scripture generally that a maleducated public had fallen into. Unhappily, Darwin's selection theory also brought him into conflict with the spirit and underlying presumption of what he intended to serve, the rational inquiry called science.

If brute struggle for survival accounts for man's emergence, and if such struggle therafter forms and governs him, the door is firmly shut not only against the Judeo-Christian (and Platonic) conception of God but also against the possibility of free or self-determining mind. This because it follows from such a theory that men's thinking not only should but willynilly does aim at survival more than truth. Darwinism deals confidence in science and rational thought in any field a potentially fatal blow.

If Darwin's theory stands, thinking becomes what Trotsky once called it, simply a manifestation of matter seeking to survive — and therefore embracing whatever ideas and pursuing whatever policies further that overriding urge. In Darwin's day few people perceived that implication of his theory, but he himself may have been one of them. In 1881 he confessed to a correspondent that he was sometimes assailed by a "horrid doubt" of the trustworthiness of any of the convictions held by minds that had "developed from the mind of the lower animals"[10] Granting his theory, given that man is only a biologically improved ape, such doubt cannot be suppressed. For it follows from Darwin's theory that we are not free to choose between ideas on the grounds of truth or falsity but are compelled by the survival urge to accept those that promote survival, be they true or not. Any arguments for their truth only rationalize that urge. And while ideas with survival value may often be true, i.e., may accurately describe reality, in circumstances easy to imagine they may be false.

Moral and religious issues quite aside, Darwin had constructed a theory that cast irremediable doubt on all thought whatever and in so doing rebounded logically against its own claim to truth. To sum up the desperate logical bind to which the theory leads: if my desire to survive determines my beliefs, I have no reason to believe that my beliefs are true—but then I have no reason to believe that they arise from such a cause. Scientifically and philosophically I am thoroughly estopped. When differences of opinion arise, the resort will be to force.

Thinking that they were championing reason against religious obscurantism, Darwin and his followers unwittingly drove the opening wedge for the distrust of reason and the indifference to "mere logic" so conspicuous in 20th-century culture. Darwinian selection theory undoubtedly paved the way for the more explicit Marxian and Freudian views of reason as the unwitting agent of blind sub-rational drives. Given Darwinism's continuing popular success, it seems no accident that our own time has witnessed increasingly explicit denials of the existence of anything properly called mind.[11]

Though Darwin all too easily shrugged off his glimpse of the stark irrationalism his theory fostered, he did try, like many present-day Darwinians, to mitigate his theory's essential ferocity. Appealing chiefly to evidence found in social insects, he argued that cooperation as well as competition might promote survival and so, along with competition, follow from and characterize the struggle for existence. That is surely true, but its effect upon his theory is disastrous: it robs the struggle for existence of the explanatory power that Darwin originally accorded it. If "struggle for existence" denotes cooperation as well as competition, it can no more explain either of them or their results than mere living can explain health or sickness. It becomes a general condition of both and hence explains neither. If nonetheless appealed to for explanation, it becomes a concept that in its opposing meanings can "explain" wholly contrary things. Such explanation, one need hardly add, seldom satisfies careful scientists.

While we shall see that Darwin sometimes leaned heavily on the ambiguity described, for the most part he gave "struggle for existence" the meaning of competition. For his theory's sake he had to. This because cooperation cannot ensure, but may well prevent, the pre-eminent success and reproduction of the fortunate individuals who according to his theory launch new species. Most of the time it was, and for his theory's sake had to be, "the great battle of life" that under the spell of an ascendant naturalism this affectionate father and husband, likeable man, and semi-invlaid insisted on. In his opinion that battle was mainly fought not between species, as Lyell had suggested, but between those creatures best suited for cooperation, members of the same species.

All six editions of the *Origin* which Darwin himself carried through devote pages to emphasizing that competition comes to apogee and exhibits its selective wisdom especially among individuals of the same species. Darwin argues that such individuals inhabit the same environment, require the same means of subsistence, and so compete most strenuously.

In *The Descent of Man*, which followed the *Origin* by about twelve years, Darwin re-emphasized his concern for individual competition with this warning:

— [man] is to advance still higher, it is to be feared that he must remain subject to a severe struggle. Otherwise . . . the more gifted men would not be more successful in the battle of life than the less gifted. Hence our normal rate of increase, though leading to many and obvious evils, must not be greatly diminished by any means. [12]

That reasoning impelled Darwin firmly to oppose all proposals to alleviate by birth control the misery of the contemporary poor. In his correspondence he expressed satisfaction at the extermination of various aboriginal races which he deemed inferior to Europeans. In the words of his biographer, Geoffrey West, popular Darwinism may have been crude, as present-day Darwinians still allege, but it was "scarecely an unfair or inaccurate presentation" of what Darwin himself had written.

Darwin's answer on a matter that deeply troubled Wallace, co-author of the original selection theory, also deserves attention. To his scientific credit, Wallace saw and admitted the difficulty of deriving man's moral sense from a brute struggle for survival. Today, thanks in part to Marx and Freud, the existence of a moral sense might simply be denied, but in Darwin's day sophistication had not attained that peak. In reply to Wallace Darwin granted that "the moral qualities are advanced . . . much more through the effects of habit, the reasoning powers, instruction, religion, etc., than through natural selection." To which he immediately added, "though to the last may safely be attributed the social instincts, which afforded the basis for the moral sense." [13]

Of course it was precisely the "social instincts" that Wallace and others could not derive from the competitive struggle that Darwin ordinarily emphasized. Relying on the ambiguity in "struggle for existence" pointed out above, Darwin derived man's moral sense from cooperation which, at this point, he declared characteristic of that struggle. Thus he used "struggle for existence" both ways, usually giving it the meaning of competition but, when necessary, the meaning of cooperation — which last, as said before, cannot ensure the pre-eminent success of those individuals with favorable variations from the norm who in his view launched new species. While Darwin appears to have accepted the Social Darwinism that follows logically from his theory, it is a fact worth more notice than usually given that he never attempted the experimental test of his theory that T. H. Huxley suggested. It seemed to Huxley that prolonged intense artificial selection might within a manageable span of time produce organisms not crossable with their parent species (the usual definition of a new species) and thus empirically prove the creative power that Darwin claimed for selection in nature. Instead of organizing this experiment, which no doubt would have failed, Darwin spent years and many chapters of the *Origin's* repeatedly revised editions in merely arguing for his theory.

From the first his claim had been, not that natural selection had actually been seen to create new species, but that in theory it could create them, and so he continued to argue against his scientific critics. Investigation of the ensuing dialogues, which occurred after the *Origin's* first publication and so attracted little public notice, turns up substantial withdrawals by leading Darwinians and Darwin himself of the original theory.

Among the most significant of these withdrawals was one forced by contemporary zoologists who wondered how organs like wings or lungs could possibly prove useful enough in the microscopic initial stages envisioned by Darwin to ensure their transmission to and further development in subsequent generations. Here Darwin defended his theory mainly by citing organs such as the giraffe's long neck and the whale's baleen whose early stages might conceivably prove useful. That, however, raised the question why other species in the same environments had not developed similar organs. There Darwin made one of his many appeals to the paucity of contemporary knowledge. Such appeals so liberally dot the later editions of the *Origin* that Darwin seems chiefly to argue that, since the truth is hidden, he cannot well be refuted. More than a generation later the geneticist August Weismann met the objection about initial stages squarely. Though a professed and foremost Darwinian, which is to say selectionist, Weismann granted that "no one who does not wish to believe in the selection value of the initial stages can be forced to do so." Weismann also wrote revealingly, "It is not upon demonstrative evidence that we rely when we champion the doctrine of selection as scientific truth; we base our arguments on quite other grounds."[14] That those grounds were philosophical has already been suggested.

Meanwhile other objections loomed and forced Darwin himself into significant retreat. One of these concerned the persistence of non-useful characteristics like peacocks' tails and the unwieldly antlers of many deer. His theory would lead us to expect these to disappear in the interest of biological efficiency. In *The Descent of Man* Darwin attempted to meet this difficulty by attributing non-useful characteristics to their supposed appeal to females of the species.[15] Once started on this new track, he ended by transferring much, in fact most, of the evolutionary burden he had initially placed on natural selection, a process instigated by scarcity of food, over to sexual selection, a process wholly different. He wrote:

> For my part I conclude that of all the causes which have led to the difference in external appearance between the races of man, and to a certain extent between man and the lower animals, sexual selection has been the most efficient. [16]

The phrase "external appearance" seems more than a little puzzling. It suggests that the differences in question are slight and superficial, but this, however true of the differences between the races of man, hardly applies to differences between fins, paws, and hands, or to those between heads with foreheads and heads without them. Factually, external differences usually indicate internal differences. Phrases equally dark and statements downright contradictory often occur when Darwin attempts to meet objections.

In any event Darwin's theory of sexual selection has fared badly in experimental tests. Few biologists take it seriously. Sexual selection of course occurs, but it does not account for the persistence of the non-useful secondary sex characteristics that Darwin hoped it could account for. Fish, birds, and other creatures artificially deprived of such characteristics find no difficulty in obtaining mates. Nor do men who shave their beards.

Darwin's early scientific critics made a point even more crucial than those so far alluded to: natural selection could at best account for what Lyell, W. C. Wells, and others had previously recognized, the *elimination* of unfit individuals and species; it could not account for the favorable variations whose accumulation, according to Darwin, produced new species. Samuel Butler, no biologist but perhaps Darwin's acutest critic, admirably summed up this pivotal point with the statement that the origin of species lay in the origin of variations.[17]

Darwin keenly felt the force of that objection. It soon led him to suggest that he had not, after all, advanced a theory of origins. In a later edition of the *Origin* and in those we read today he wrote that he had not meant to present natural selection as an "active power" originating favorable variations—though he surely had presented it as an active power originating species and accounting for evolution. Only a year after the *Origin* had first appeared he wrote to Lyell, "Talking of 'natural selection', if I had to commence *de novo* I would have used 'natural preservation'."[18] But that, too, raised a problem. As he wrote in another letter, mere preservation of favorable variations would seem a "truism," and a truism was not what he thought he had discovered.[19]

Moreover he had used "preservation" in the very title of his book. In the full title a basic confusion of origin with preservation stands out unmistakably. That full title reads: *The Origin of Species By Means of Natural Selection or The Preservation of Favored Races in the Struggle for Life*. Origin or preservation? The two are different things, no more to be joined by an equating "or" than creation and conservation. On that confusion, on the notion that the origin of new species was somehow explained by the preservation of their component variations, Darwin's whole theory with its huge and shaping influence on modernity—its raw naturalism, its latent denial of the integrity of reason—was built.

What Darwin had in all innocence constructed was a theory that not only rebounded against its own claim to truth but one that also made the problem the solution. His theory took the explicandum as a premise of the explanation. That explicandum, as Butler perceived and stated, was the emergence of the new forms that Darwin called variations. Without these natural selection would have nothing to select. And granted these, the natural selection theory does shrink toward truism: it asserts that new forms fitted to survive will survive . . . . Equally important, from the mere preservation of a favorable variation it does not follow that the variation will develop further. Its further development depends on the emergence of further variations of the same nature.

Whence come the favorable new forms? That was the question, and no selection theory can answer it. It should be a caution to us all that under the spell of a naturalistic Progressism confidently seeking vindication and deployment in every field, most of the educated public accepted as an explanation of spectacularly new forms of life the constant and continuing emergence of slightly new forms. Logically, it was like explaining the origin of the airplane by the unexplained origin of its engine, wings, and propeller. What such a theory states may be undeniable — the components named did indeed come into being — but the theory takes for granted what most of all requires explanation.

To account for favorable variations, the crux of the problem of progressive evolution, Darwin fell back on Lamarckian processes of use and disuse and the inheritance of acquired characteristics. He is often lauded for having rejected these, but in later editions of the *Origin* he insisted that he had always recognized them.[20] In his *Variation of Plants and Animals Under Domestication* of 1866 he approvingly cited alleged examples of Lamarckism, including a cow that after accidentally losing one horn gave birth to calves similarly deprived.

Darwin's defense of his theory by dubious arguments instead of by organizing the experimental test that Huxley had suggested does not diminis   stature as an observer. Many of his observations of plants and animals hold respected places in our present store of knowledge. But his arguments, along with his confusion of origin with preservation and his theory's logical rebound against its own claim to truth, stand in startling contrast to his reputation as a theorist or thinker.

In *The Descent of Man* Darwin wrote that he had "perhaps attributed too much to the action of natural selection or survival of the fittest."[21] That book's full title, *The Descent of Man and Selection in Relation to Sex*, indicates the weight that Darwin finally gave to sexual selection. Yet even that major, and unsuccessful, revision of his original theory left him with a large residuum of non-useful characteristics wholly unrelated to sex. In the end, in a late edition of the *Descent*, he finally added to sexual selection the working of "unknown causes."[22] There indeed he hit the truth, and there, since the unknown causes frequently did duty as the effective causes, we have a final admission of puzzlement in the area he had initially claimed to explain. There we have in effect a withdrawal of his theory.

In truth Darwin's predecessors, who had recognized all the components of his theory, including natural selection, without finding in them an explanation of evolution, had said all that rightly could be said about the origin of species, given the knowledge available at the time. Darwin's contribution lay in claiming for natural selection a primary and unlimited creative power in addition to its secondary pruning power. And in that, which made the tremendous splash whose moral and philosophic waves still rock us, Charles Darwin was thoroughly mistaken.

*   *   *

Led in our century by such men as R. A. Fisher, Julian Huxley, G. G. Simpson, and Theodosius Dobzhansky,

Darwinian biologists have identified Darwin's unknown causes of evolution with the gene mutations and genetic shuffling that occur in the reproductive process. These account for the heritable new variations that Darwin's selection theory could not account for. Curiously enough, we owe our knowledge of genes and inheritance not to any evangelist of philosophical naturalism but primarily to an Augustinian monk, Gregor Mendel, who in the 1860's subjected to mathematical analysis the results of his experiments with peas in a monastery garden. To pick up Mendel's rigorously reasoned "Experiments in Plant Hybridization" after reading Darwin's anecdotal arguments is to enter almost a new universe of thought.[23] The monk was a consummate scientist.

Where Darwin had conceived inheritance as a simple blending of parental constitutions, Mendel's work revealed inheritance's particulate nature and its units' (genes) unblendability and usual stability.[24] Hoping to gain the notice of the ruling mandarins of science, Mendel sent a copy of his paper to Darwin. Darwin never cut its pages.

As Darwinians now see it, gene mutations and Mendelian inheritance provide the raw material of evolution, i.e., Darwin's variations, and natural selection then screens these for usefulness in a struggle for survival. Thus Mendelian, i.e., genetic, processes are prime constituents of the modern Darwinian, often styled "synthetic" (selection plus genetics), theory of evolution. And their discovery, Darwinians contend, clears up Darwin's difficulties and so proves Darwin's original theory essentially correct. To this contention two major demurrers must be entered.

First, if we momentarily set aside Darwin's espousal of the general concept of evolution and consider only the *explanation* of evolution that he himself contributed, namely creative natural selection, the impressive but by no means unanimous support that the above contention enjoys among biologists will not prevent us from finding it a plain non-sequitur. What Darwinians surely mean and what should be allowed them is that natural selection does often eliminate non-useful or unfavorable characteristics— though, as we have seen, not always. Darwinians also mean that beyond Genesis' figurative description of creation, and in lieu of the fictitious process of inheritance of acquired characteristics, genetic processes accounting for heritable variations and so for descent with modification have been found. But it is these gratuitous processes, not a war of nature decided by animal cunning and brute force, that account for new variations and thereby offer some insight into the origin of species. And these processes differ categorically from anything that Darwin imagined.

Our second demurrer to the contention that genetic discoveries have vindicated Darwin's original theory takes into consideration Darwin's espousal of evolution itself. The demurrer rests upon modern biologists' rejection of the original Leibnizian or Progressist conception of evolution, which Darwin shared and fixed in the public mind. Despite occasional recognition that evolution could be regressive, as in parasites, Darwin took the Progressist conception as his datum and felt that natural selection explained it. "Although," he wrote, "we have no good evidence of . . . an innate tendency toward progressive development, yet this necessarily follows . . . through the action of natural selection."[25] Modern Darwinians have told us that the facts run otherwise.

Julian Huxley has observed that birds have not improved as flying mechanisms for some fifteen million years, and that ants have enjoyed, or endured, an even longer stability. In this regard bacteria have easily out-distanced both. Many similar facts make it clear that, whatever its cause or explanation, evolution has seldom produced new forms that have continued to evolve in a direction that might be called progressive. Overall evolutionary progress, Simpson has written, "can no longer be considered as characteristic of evolution or even as inherent in it."[26]

The record in the rocks shows new and higher forms occasionally appearing, with puzzling suddenness, but it seldom if ever shows such forms' subsequent progress toward greater intelligence or control over mode of life. Instead, it shows new forms' mere adaptive radiation into various ecological niches and occasional improvements in basic specialties like predation or swimming, which improvements lock the organism into those specializations and so make them evolutionary dead ends. While evolution in the sense of adaptive radiation or diversification of basic forms no doubt still persists, as when insects develop resistance to pesticides, even Darwinians now admit the probability that all basic forms except man reached evolutionary dead ends long ago. According to Huxley, this appears an established fact.[27]

While man seems so far to have escaped such a dead end (increasing dependence on an artificial environment could indicate the contrary), physical anthropologists tell us that in actual fact man's physical habit, which includes his brain, has not significantly changed over a period that varies in recent estimates from fifty thousand to several hundred thousand years. Striking a mean, Rene Dubos not long ago advised the American Association for the Advancement of Science that man's genetic endowment had not changed over the last hundred thousand years.[28] In

Darwin's and Progressism's heyday Rudolph Virchow pressed the same point, but gained no hearing. In the original Darwinian, Progressist sense of the word, evolution appears long ago to have come to a halt.

Such evolution as can result from genetic shuffling in ordinary parenthood of course continues, but modern Darwinism makes mutations the real engines of evolutionary change. According to modern Darwinism, a change that in the future might produce a species as advanced from *Homo sapiens* as *Homo sapiens* is from half-brained hominids would require far more than shuffling of our existing gene pool; it would require an enormous number of viable mutations, each one, however tiny, as indisputably a novelty as our opposable thumb or capacity for symbolic thought. Such mutations have not occurred, which means, *contra* Darwin, that man has not for ages been an evolving creature.

It may be objected that on an evolutionary time scale the period considered above has been short, but on that scale several hundred thousand years is not short. Even fifty thousand years constitutes an appreciable fraction, one twentieth, of the million years that Darwinians usually cite as the time required for evolution to fix a new species. In this area we must guard against the proclivity, induced by the very conception of a still-continuing evolution, to imagine that over an immense span of time anything necessary to validate that conception will come to pass. Giorgio de Santillana, M.I.T.'s distinguished historian of science, has observed that constant repetition of "those soporific words 'gradually' and 'step by step' " confers a spurious credibility on any imagined change whatever.[29] The French biologist, Lecomte du Noüy, put the matter with Gallic clarity: if nothing happens in one year, multiplication by a million still yields nothing.

Today the statement, first made by Wallace, that in man biological evolution has given way to and been replaced by cultural evolution comes with increasing frequency from professedly Darwinian biologists. Julian Huxley, who might be described as a Darwinian's Darwinian, wrote in 1959:

> A few million years ago, it now appears, living matter had reached the limits of material and physical development; only the possibilities of mind remained largely unrealized . . . . [Finally early man] initiated a new phase of evolution, the human or psychosocial phase. . . .[30]

That and similar statements by equally respected modern Darwinians present psychosocial evolution, popularly understood as social and even moral progress, as a *replacement* for the biological evolution that to many moderns somehow seems psychosocial evolution's support and guarantee. In the new view that support and guarantee has been withdrawn. Biology no longer purports to give us reason to think that man's growing mastery of physical nature will be exercised by people more intelligent or virtuous than our remote forebears.

In the area we are now considering Simpson differs from Huxley and argues that significant biological evolution must still continue. But Simpson goes on to observe that today man's biological evolution is overlaid and dominated, which means directed, by psychosocial evolution. Thus here, too, the roles envisioned in Darwin's day stand reversed, with biological evolution now seen as an extension or function of psychosocial evolution. In Simpson's view as clearly as in Huxley's, biological evolution no longer guarantees man's unending progress.[31]

Biologists now recognize the progressive evolution of only a few forms of life in the past, the final specialization of other forms, the extinction of countless once-successful forms, and, what most concerns us, a long-continued absence of significant change in man. Man was man when woolly mammoths roamed the Pleistocene wilderness, and man is biologically the same man now. The science of genetics has made it clear that the constitution of living things has been determined by their germ plasm and has not been susceptible to change by human effort or social institutions. This writes—or should write—Finis both to Social Darwinism and to the Marxist notion that socialist society will improve the human species.[32]

Given the difference between finding the root cause of evolution in a selective war of nature and finding it in gratuitous mutations, and given the difference between an evolution still driving toward perfection and an evolution that has largely ended, we must demur when Darwinians assert the essential correctness of Darwin's original theory. Their own testimony speaks against it. Essentially correct was only the truism that variations fitted to survive would survive. Modern Darwinism rejects original Darwinism's cardinal notion of creative natural selection.

Now we ask if modern Darwinism, i.e., the synthetic theory, constitutes a satisfactory theory of evolution.

Like original Darwinism, the modern formulation undercuts its own claim to truth. This because the new theory follows Darwin's original one in conceiving new forms of life to be the results of gradual accumulations of countless tiny variations, each one of which wins its way into the evolutionary stream by proving useful in the struggle for survival. Failing such usefulness, a variation vanishes. The irrationalist consequence comes out with brutal clarity in modern Darwinism's latest dilation, sociobiology. The Harvard sociobiologist E. O. Wilson writes in his *On Human*

Nature, "The intellect was not constructed to understand atoms or even to understand itself but to promote the survival of human genes." Wilson also writes, "The human mind is a device for survival and reproduction, and reason is just one of its various techniques."[33] Selection theory old or new cannot dispel the radical distrust that Darwin himself sometimes, and rightly, felt toward mind that had "developed from the mind of the lower animals."

Modern Darwinism faces a difficulty of another sort in the origin of life itself or of the *first* species, with which the selection process presumably began. Here we must recognize that, in Simpson's words, "much more is required in the development of even the simplest living organism than simply a creation of organic complex molecules." Simpson lists as further requirements the ability to adapt, to acquire and store information, and to reproduce.[34] That a chance tumbling together of inanimate molecules should meet these requirements, as Darwinians conceive, seems fantastically improbable. Conversely, if geologic ages ago the molecular dice overcame that improbability, why have they not overcome it since? Why do they not overcome it frequently? These difficulties impelled Dobzhansky to a curious and significant locution. He termed the origin of life one of two great "transcendences in the evolutionary process."[35] Which evidently means that life resulted from causes other than random mutation and natural selection.

Modern Darwinism also fails to resolve the difficulties posed by the persistence of non-useful characteristics and by the non-usefulness of new organs such as wings or lungs in what it conceives to be their microscopic initial stages. Sir Karl Popper has tried to solve the latter difficulty by suggesting a "genetic dualism" that posits the existence of genes for wants or aims as well as for anatomical form. This would allow for behavioral as well as anatomical mutations and might serve brilliantly in selection theory's long grapple with the origin of the eye: a behavioral mutation inclining an organism to make use of a light-sensitive spot on its anatomy might account for such a spot's transmission to later generations.[36] But it is hard to imagine how the beginnings of wings or lungs, not useful at all in their initial stages, would be transmitted even if an organism wanted to fly or breathe air. Toward the solution of such difficulties, and of the persistence of characteristics without potential usefulness, little progress seems to have been made since August Weismann candidly acknowledged selection theory's lack of demonstrative evidence.

In agreeing with Darwin's original view of evolution as a slow accumulation of tiny variations, i.e., mutations, modern Darwinism would seem, like Darwin's original theory, to require the record in the rocks to consist of constantly changing transitional forms. In fact, such forms seldom if ever appear. Though hopelessly in error in denying the earth's great age, "creation scientists" rightly insist on this: the fossil record consists overwhelmingly of fixed and definable species, genera, and higher taxonomic categories that appear suddenly and differ sharply from one another. Trying to account for this, Darwinians have argued that natural selection may have operated rapidly at some periods, leaving few transition forms, and slowed to a halt at other periods, leaving the observed abundance of stable forms. They have also argued that selection may have operated in small isolated populations that left few fossils but then spread rapidly. The notion that natural selection should so conveniently adjust itself to Darwinian theory bears the marks of argument *ad hoc*.

In any event, no instances of small mutations accumulating into large and striking evolutionary changes have actually been observed, whether in gardens, breeding pens or bottles, or in the fossil record. In laboratories, however intensively subjected to artificial selection, fruit flies remain fruit flies and no more change into house flies than dogs change into cats. In both the plant and animal worlds selective breeders find that changes do not accumulate or develop indefinitely. Living creatures do not seem infinitely malleable. At a certain point change comes up against a "species barrier," and the plant or animal under selective breeding either reverts to type or grows sterile or dies.

Mindful of that and other difficulties a generation ago, the eminent geneticist Richard Goldschmidt styled modern Darwinism's mutations, which are Darwin's variations, "micro-mutations" and declared them able to account only for "micro-evolution," i.e., evolution that did not proceed beyond the limits of the species. Such mutations could account for a bigger dog or a bird's or plant's change of color, but they could not account for a new species evolving from an old one. They would leave species as Lyell had found them a century-and-a-half ago, "variable but only within certain fixed limits."

Goldschmidt wrote:

> I may challenge the adherents of the [synthetic] views, which we are discussing here, to try to explain the evolution of the following features by accumulation and selection of small mutants: hair in mammals, feathers in birds, segmentation of arthropods and vertebrates . . . compound eyes, blood circulation . . . poison apparatus of snakes . . . and, finally, primary chemical differences like hemoglobin vs. hemocyanin (in presumably filiated species).[37]

That challenge has not been met.

The same and similar objections to modern Darwinism had been put forward some years earlier by du Noüy:

> By no effort of the imagination can we actually conceive the passage from monocellular beings to Metazoa, from asexual generations to sexual generations, from blood pigment containing copper to blood pigment containing iron . . . . These transformations . . . have absolutely nothing to do with the ends of adaptation [survival] and are fundamental as far as evolution is concerned . . . . We must recognize the fact that [Darwinian processes] are incapable of explaining an immense number of facts which still remain absolutely mysterious and constitute as many insurmountable obstacles . . . .[36]

Goldschmidt, du Noüy, and others have found selection theory, however revised and augmented by genetics, unable to account for many other emergences and discontinuities. And must not everyone find any theory of selection-for-use embarrassed by the emergence and long persistence of the present human brain? Neurophysiologists tell us that about half of that organ is seldom or never used.

Du Noüy sought to solve the difficulties he emphasized by going beyond selection theory to a "telefinalism" that postulated a preordained purpose in nature's workings. His fellow biologists found that appeal to an Aristotelian final cause unacceptably metaphysical, an open invitation to religion. Goldschmidt clove to selection and suggested, as the cause of "macro-evolution," i.e., of large and striking evolutionary change, a process he called "systemic mutation." This consisted in a wholesale "re-patterning of the chromosomes, which results in a new genetic system," colloquially a "hopeful monster." But Goldschmidt granted that no such huge mutation had been observed or seemed likely to prove anything but fatal. Though different, the objections to Goldschmidt's suggestion appear quite as strong as those to conventional gradualist Darwinism.

In the case that most concerns us, man's, we have seen that nothing promising a new species, in fact no significant change, has occurred for about one hundred thousand years, perhaps much longer. Fossil and other discoveries keep pushing man's first appearance farther and farther back toward the start of the Pleistocene, beyond which no human fossils are found. For example, the use of controlled fire, probably with the burial of the dead the surest evidence of man's existence, now seems to have occurred about a million years earlier than has been thought.[39] Carlton Coon and some other anthropologists have asserted that *Homo sapiens* once co-existed with the small-brained hominids that still other anthropologists have called his ancestors. Giorgio de Santillana's investigation of prehistoric myth has convinced him that tens of thousands of years ago man had already accumulated and was transmitting to his descendants a vast and systematic body of astronomical knowledge.[40] All indicates that man originated earlier and, in view of humans' non-existence before the Pleistocene, more rapidly than present-day Darwinian theory can easily, if at all, accommodate.

For all his assertive Darwinism, Jacob Bronowski eventually wrote that man had emerged with "breakneck" speed.[41] Loren Eiseley has called the emergence of man's mind, clearly man's most distinctive feature, "explosively short."[42] Dobzhansky has called the same event a second "transcendence" in the evolutionary process.

Meanwhile molecular biologists, aware of the extreme complexity and interdependence of hereditary materials, are finding it increasingly difficult to imagine an evolution governed by selection. Nearly all genes produce multiple effects. Organisms are delicately coordinated structures of these multiple effects and so seem unlikely to respond to environmental pressures that may favor one effect but ignore the balance and coordination of the whole.

That only simple forms of life appear in early rock strata, that more complex and highly organized forms appear in later strata, and that embryos of complex species pass through phases resembling simpler species, constitutes impressive evidence for the general conception of evolution, i.e., for the descent of many forms of life from forms strikingly different. The fossil record alone seems proof that simple forms antedated complex forms and, aided by mutations, engendered them. But since many of the simplest forms still survive, the fossil record does not prove complex forms' superior survivability. Nor does it prove that complex forms resulted from slow Darwinian selection of small mutations. For that last, Darwinians would have to present us with enormously long and substantially unbroken sequences of tiny steps from early species to later and more complex species. Despite strenuous search, Darwinians have not found such sequences. In view of the limits to plant and animal variation mentioned above, they seem unlikely ever to find them. The one that has been most commonly cited, the sequence from *eohippus* to the horse, has been found to be a tangle of perplexities.[45] No one doubts that new forms appear in the paleontological record, but thereafter both they and the old forms seem fixed within stable limits.

That no compelling alternative exists to the modern Darwinian or synthetic theory of evolution might be called negative evidence for it. In all fields scientists commonly and probably rightly hold to theories that, despite minor difficulties, possess large explanatory-predictive power. Darwinian theory, however, yields no predictions. Like historians' explanations of past and unrepeatable events it is postdictive only. And its explanatory failures seem greater and more numerous than its explanatory successes. Its failures have become increasingly difficult to consider minor anomalies that future workers in the field will somehow clear up.

However altered and augmented by genetics, selection theory has not provided us with a tenable theory of evolution. Today, in what seems like desperation, some selectionists have revived theories of pangenesis. These hold that all the cells in the body, not only the germ cells, generate self-reproductive material and thus permit or ensure the inheritance of acquired characteristics. Evidence for this seems absent.

Certain paleontologists and molecular biologists have taken a direction that may prove more promising. Admitting the failure of Darwinians' century-long search for transition forms, these theorists accept the known fossil record as substantially correct. According to Gunther S. Stent of the University of California at Berkeley, "most new species made their appearance suddenly, full blown, and without any traces of the 'missing links' essential to traditional Darwinism." Stent also writes:

> For most of the eons of its existence a species changes very little, but occasionally the species suddenly sports a variant form that differs from the parent so substantially that parent and variant no longer interbreed.[44]

This "punctuational" hypothesis, as it is called, takes the direction Goldschmidt took but does not go so far. It accounts for the origin of new species not by sudden muta-

tions of entire genetic systems but by several large mutations occurring suddenly within existing systems. By
granting creationists' strongest point, the absence of transition forms in the fossil record, the punctuational hypothesis
might bridge much of the distance between creationists and
evolutionists. What arouses creationists' hostility to the
idea of evolution itself seems at bottom their conceiving it as
Darwin conceived it and a just perception of its immorality
and irreligion when so conceived. By totally discarding
Darwin's notion of the slow step-by-step accumulation of
"infinitesimally small" and useful variations, the latest
evolutionary hypothesis greatly reduces natural selection's
evolutionary role.

While modern Darwinism rightly denies natural selection the creative power that Darwin attributed to it, punctuationalism goes on also to deny what modern Darwinism
still affirms, that natural selection screens and in effect
models each minute biological novelty as it appears. Steven
M. Stanley of Johns Hopkins University writes in *The New
Evolutionary Timetable* that while natural selection eliminates
maladapted forms, the result is only to stabilize or relieve of
freaks new and viable species when these, suddenly possessing a variety of new features, appear.[45] This would mean
that new species could possess, in addition to survivability,
features irrelevant to survivability. A mind not dominated
by the urge to survive, a mind free to pursue truth or good,
might be just such a feature. Punctuationalism might allow
for the existence of the free and responsible mind that any
theory of evolution must allow for if we are to consider it or
any other idea a product of rational thought. Thus punctuationalism might rescue us from the irrationalism and
immorality in which, with huge effect on 20th-century
thought and conduct, evolution theory has been mired.

So much said, however, it must be admitted that no genetic mechanism capable of accomplishing the sudden speciation envisioned by punctuationalism has been discovered.

The plain truth is that we do not possess a theory of evolution that recommends itself to critical minds. Every hypothesis suggested comes hard aground on an unyielding reef of logic or empirical fact or both.

Evolutionists commonly insist that our ignorance of the "how" or method of evolution in no way casts doubt on what they call the "fact" of evolution. But in truth the real or imagined method of evolution gives the word most of its meaning. Until we discover that method the statement "evolution is a fact" means little more than what Augustine recognized more than a millenium-and-a-half ago: that the six days of the Genesis creation story cannot be taken literally.

Those slumberous words "gradually" and "step-by-step" have lulled us into unthinking acceptance of a concept that demands some fundamental thought. By "evolution" do we mean simply a re-arrangement of previously existing materials, a development or unfolding of something that in some sense existed before it became observable, as a chicken exists in an egg? If so, do we then attribute some spark of life and even mind to the gases out of which astrophysicists in company with evolutionists tell us that life and mind eventually evolved—do we accept panpsychism? Or do we mean by "evolution" the emergence of things altogether novel, as in our solar system at least, life and mind (Dobzhansky's "transcendences") appear to be? If so, we admit unpredictable and unintelligible discontinuities in, or invasions of, nature; we surrender hope of finding an intelligible order in nature and seem to admit the operation of non-natural and even supernatural power. Neither of these alternatives fits easily into science as science is now conceived.

What seems most worthy of attention in the ground that we have covered are not only the logical and empirical failures of original Darwinism and of its re-formulation in the modern synthetic theory; it is also that many of Darwinism's failures were perceived in Darwin's day, sometimes by Darwin himself, that additional ones are perceived in our day, and that nevertheless educators and opinion-makers have enthusiastically propagated Darwinism and most of the educated public has enthusiastically accepted it. Pretty obviously, something other than pure zeal for knowledge has been at work. The concluding chapter of this book will seek to identify it.

We simply do not know how living creatures came to be as they are, and it is certain that no explanation of their origins will ever carry the authority of actually observed fact. However well supported by geology, the fossil record, and embryology, evolution remains an inference, and one whose actual meaning is far from clear. Our little knowledge does, however, allow two substantial statements:

First, man has for ages been as fixed within the limits of a basic biological nature, a genotype, as ancient and medieval thinkers presumed he was. He has not for ages been an evolving creature. This means that, insofar as ancient and medieval teachings about man and society presumed such fixity they, as opposed to teaching born of the notion of continuing human evolution, hold true today and fit such creatures as ourselves.

Second, however man came into being, he did so by virtue of a process different from the one imagined by

Darwin. Acknowledgement of the empirical and logical failures of Darwinism, i.e., of the theory that natural selection causes evolution, removes the support that biology once seemed to offer philosophical naturalism. It also goes far to relieve us of the radical distrust of the human mind's integrity that Darwin unwittingly planted in modernity.

Notes on Chapter I

1. Ludwig Edelstein, *The Idea of Progress in Classical Antiquity*, 1967, establishes the fact of a Graeco-Roman idea of Progress all but identical with the modern idea. Aristotle, *Physics*, Bk. II, ch. 8, makes plain the currency in Aristotle's time of a selection theory of evolution like Darwin's. Aristotle rejected it.

2. Cited in Geoffrey West, *Charles Darwin*, London, 1937, p. 252.

3. Lyell, *Principles*, 3rd ed., vol. II, p. 391.

4. *Loc. cit.*, p. 267.

5. For Darwin's summary of his theory see *The Origin of Species and the Descent of Man*, Modern Library ed., n.d., p. 98. Subsequent quotations from the *Origin* and the *Descent* are from the same edition, which prints Darwin's version of 1872.

6. *Origin and Descent*, p. 374.

7. Hitler must be counted among Social Darwinists. Hitler's press chief, Otto Dietrich, observed in his *Hitler*, 1955, p. 19, "Hitler took such principles as the struggle for existence, the survival of the fittest and strongest, as a new imperative." Nazi Darwinism has also been attested by Hannah Arendt in *The Origins of Totalitarianism*, Alan Bullock in *Hitler: A Study in Tyranny*, and T. Jarman, *The Rise and Fall of Nazi Germany*.

8. T. H. Huxley and Julian Huxley, *Touchstone for Ethics*, 1947, p. 91.

9. On Augustine's view and Milton's influence see Henry Cotterill, *Does Science Aid Faith in Regard to Creation?*, London, 1883, pp. 63-73. These writers translate and quote Augustine, *De Genesi contra Manicheos*, Bk. I, sec. 7, and Augustine, *De Genesi ad litteram*, Bk. V, secs. 5, 23, which elsewhere do not seem to have been translated into English. See also Henry Fairfield Osborn, *From the Greeks to Darwin*, 1929, pp. 106-12, which highlights Suarez' influence.

10. Letter to W. Graham in *The Life and Letters of Charles Darwin*, Francis Darwin, ed., 1898, vol. I, p. 284. See also vol. I, pp. 312-13. Essentially the same problem impelled Sir Karl Popper to call for "a new theory of evolution, and a new model for the organism." Cf. Popper, *Objective Knowledge*, Oxford, 1972, p. 232.

11. E.g., Herbert Simon in *The American Scholar* (Spring, 1966): 220, and Keith Gunderson in *Inquiry* (Winter, 1959): 406f. Quite a contrary view is expressed by the eminent neurophysiologist Wilder Penfield in *The Mystery of the Mind: A Critical Study of Consciousness and the Human Brain* (Princeton, NJ: Princeton University Press, 1975).

12. *Origin and Descent*, p. 919. See also p. 60.

13. *Origin and Descent*, p. 919. See also pp. 478-79.

14. Weismann' article, "The Selection Theory," in *Darwin and Modern Science*, A. C. Seward ed., 1909, p. 27. Gertrude Himmelfarb, *Darwin and the Darwinian Revolution*, 1962, p. 336, highlights Darwin's frequent appeals to contemporary ignorance in lieu of evidence.

15. Stephen Jay Gould, *Ever Since Darwin*, 1977, p. 79 attempts a Darwinian explanation of unwieldy antlers, calling them useful in attracting females and eliminating harmful combat among males in favor of mere ritualistic display. Outdoorsmen have frequently watched young, lightly-antlered males impregnate females while older, heavily-antlered males engage in sometimes fatal combat.

16. *Origin and Descent*, p. 908.

17. Butler, *Life and Habit*, vol. IV of Shrewsbury edition of Butler's works, p. 215.

18. Letter of Sept. 28, 1860, in *Life and Letters, op. cit.*, vol. II, p. 138.

19. Letter of June 6, 1860, in *Life and Letters*, vol. II, p. 111. See also letter of July 5, 1866.

20. *Origin and Descent*, p. 160, *passim*.

21. *Ibid.*, p. 441.

22. *Ibid.*, p. 910. See also "dimly seen causes," pp. 156, 159, 556, *passim*.

23. See Mendel's paper in *Mendel Centenary: Genetics, Development, and Evolution*, Roland M. Nardone ed., 1968.

24. Blending of parental characteristics would in fact produce universal homogeneity, thus *preventing* evolution!

25. *Origin and Descent*, p. 180

26. Simpson, *The Meaning of Evolution*, 1953, p. 178.

27. Huxley's essay, "Darwinism Today" in Huxley, *Man and the Modern World*.

28. Dubos' Phi Beta Kappa-Sigma Chi address of 1965, printed in *The American Scholar* (Spring, 1965).

29. Giorgio de Santillana and Hertha von Dechend, *Hamlet's Mill*, 1969, p. 68f. See, for example, *Origin and Descent*, p. 82, *passim*.

30. Huxley's essay, "The Future of Man" in *Bulletin of Atomic Scientists*, December, 1959, p. 402.

31. Simpson, *op. cit.*, p. 344. Meanwhile Simpson still claims creative power for natural selection. But while that process can produce results affecting the environment to the point of deciding the survival value of subsequent mutations, any creativity attributable to it is conditional on and derived from mutations, not primary.

32. Disturbed by genetics' anti-Marxian drift, Stalin liquidated the geneticist Vavilov and promoted the clown Lysenko.

33. Wilson, *On Human Nature*, 1978, pp. 2, 195, *passim.*

34. Simpson, *This View of Life: The World of an Evolutionist*, 1964.

35. Dobzhansky, *The Biology of Ultimate Concern*, 1967, p. 32.

36. Popper, *Objective Knowledge, op. cit.*, pp. 272, 283.

37. Goldschmidt, *The Material Basis of Evolution*, 1960, pp. 6-7.

38. DuNoüy, *Human Destiny*, 1947, p. 50.

39. Cf. *New York Times*, Nov. 14, 1981, p. 1.

40. *Hamlet's Mill, op. cit.*, p. 68f.

41. *The American Scholar* (Spring, 1972):201.

42. Eiseley, *The Immense Journey*, 1946, p. 91. See also *Time and Stratigraphy in the Evolution of Man*, National Academy of Sciences, 1965, p. 69f., where Eiseley finds need of terms as curious as "preadaptation" and "orthoselection." Preadaptation occurs *before* the environment favors it. Orthoselection hints, at least, at the teleology that scientists reject.

43. Cf. Norman Macbeth, *Darwin Retried*, p. 15.

44. *New York Times Book Review*, January 17, 1982, p. 3.

45. *Loc. cit.*, p. 121, *passim.*

Chapter II
Marxism

It cannot be said of Marx, as it can of Darwin, that he was a careless or bumbling thinker. Steeped in philosophy at the universities of Berlin and Bonn, a Doctor of Philosophy who impressed those who knew him with the force and cogency of his speech, Marx dealt in ideas with a surer hand than most of his followers and many of his critics. He fashioned a doctrine that, whatever its relation to reality, achieved coherence and testified to abounding mental energy. On occasion Marx was also master of a vigorous prose.

Yet when Marx died in 1883 his doctrine had reached few people outside the then-small socialist movement. Endless wrestle with his economic theories had allowed him to present only the first volume of his intended masterwork, *Capital*, to even that restricted audience. It was only in the 1890's, when the socialist audience had grown larger, that what still bears heavily upon the world, Marx's socio-historical teaching, Marx's macrosociology, reached intellectuals generally and the educated public. At that time, however, it fell on ground prepared by Darwinism to receive it. Since then it has taken root, branched, and blossomed more widely than commonly suspected.

Surveying sociology in the 1930's, the historian J. T. Shotwell observed that the social dynamics taught in universities rested on foundations laid by Marx. Not long after World War II the sociologist R. K. Merton of Columbia University remarked with satisfaction the indubitably Marxian "prevailing view . . . that social location [class] determines the perspectives entering into perceptions, beliefs, and ideas."[1] Launching a discussion of social theory in 1973, Daniel Bell of Harvard paid homage to Marx as the thinker who had directed living social theorists' first steps.[2] Today, avowed Marxists abound in university faculties. No fewer than seven printings of a college textbook, *Alienation: The Marxist Conception of Man in Capitalist Society*, by a leading American Marxist have left a Marxist deposit in many thousands of college-educated minds.

Though sometimes surprising to taxpayers supporting higher education and to parents struggling to meet tuition fees, assumptions and concepts derived from Marx often guide discussion of society and history in American colleges and universities. Often they are not attributed to Marx but are presented simply as the beginning of social and historical wisdom. Even anti-Marxists frequently use the word "capitalism" to denote a type of society instead of only a type of economy within and answerable to a society, which suggests acceptance of Marx's contention that economics determines all. Meanwhile the attention paid to such earlier writers on history and society as Plato, Vico, and de Tocqueville, or to such later non-Marxists as Max Weber, Ortega y Gasset, and Pitirim Sorokin, does not compare with the respectful attention paid to Marx.

But much has happened since Marx's day, and much of it, from rising wages in the West to the Russian, Chinese, and other Marxist revolutions and their outcomes, has cruelly strained Marx's doctrine. Events have not fallen out as Marx expected. In consequence, out of a fealty to Marx for which this book's Conclusion will offer an explanation, Marxists of various stamp and degree have so variously interpreted, edited, and selectively propagated the original doctrine that today no Marxist's or semi-Marxist's account of it often satisfies any other Marxist or semi-Marxist.

Following the failure of the industrial workers' insurrections that flared across Europe in 1848, and following the success of Ferdinand Lassalle's parliamentary efforts for German workers, many Marxists came to view not the overthrow but the capture of existing institutions as the best way of realizing Marx's radical aims. In Germany this tendency crystallized in the Social Democratic Party's Gotha Program of 1875. Though harshly criticized for its gradualism by Marx himself, that gradualism gained and in essentials has held the allegiance of many West European and American Marxists, who often style themselves Social Democrats.

Early in the 20th century, however, Marx's own Marxism still retained adherents, among them Nicolai Lenin, and in 1917 Lenin's triumph in Russia recalled intellectuals' attention to Marx as the author of the *Communist Manifesto* and a dedicated revolutionary. As late as the 1930's, with Stalin firmly established as Lenin's successor, the American *belletrist* Edmund Wilson pronounced revolutionary Russia "the moral top of the world where the light never really goes out."

Still later, when the realities of life under Marxism-Leninism could not be blinked, Marx the apocalyptic communist and father of the Russian Revolution went out of intellectual fashion. His place was taken by a humanist and philosophical Marx discovered in Marx's early writings and felt to have been betrayed by Lenin and Stalin both. Today, in universities especially, one may hear the credal statement, "I am not a communist. I am a Marxist." Meanwhile in political sloughs and backwaters Trotskyite, Anarcho-Surrealist, Third-World Liberationist, and various New Left Marxist cults contend against one another, and occasionally damn the Kremlin almost as heatedly as they damn America.

Given the existence of so many varying Marxisms, it will be useful to trace the development of Marx's thought from his initial impulse as a thinker. We shall see that, despite partisan appeals, pro-Marx or anti-Marx, to an early Marx or to a later Marx, to a humanist or a totalitarian Marx, Karl Marx himself steered a steady course.

Born in 1818 in the Prussian-governed city of Trier to well-to-do parents, Marx absorbed from a father and teachers sympathetic to the French Enlightenment the naturalistic Progressism that later in his lifetime Darwinian evolution theory seemed to vindicate. At the University of Berlin, to which his father sent him after a year at Bonn that Marx devoted as much to scorning "philistines" as to his studies, Marx encountered and embraced the philosophy of Hegel. This philosophy posited an Idea or Spirit of freedom that over centuries and millenia increasingly realized itself in political institutions and states.

Physically strong and handsome, often studying and writing philosophy through the night, and boundlessly self-confident, young Marx became a leading member of a student circle of Young Hegelians. Unlike Hegel himself, these young men directed especially against religion Hegel's perception of the historicity and hence impermanence and eventual replacement of once-dominant ideas.

When Marx came to write his doctoral dissertation in 1841, he raised to an intensity characteristic of him the atheism that had never been far below the surface of the French Enlightenment and that he and his friends had seen furthered in Germany by Richard Strauss and Ludwig Feuerbach. In his *Life of Jesus* Strauss had pronounced *man* "the divine one," while Feuerbach's polemical *Essence of Christianity* had declared the Judeo-Christian God a projection into the heavens of man's own best self. In the Introduction to his dissertation Marx went further. He did more than declare his disbelief in the Judeo-Christian God; he declared war against every form of transcendental belief or piety. Viewing himself as the philosophic spokesman of enlightened mankind, he wrote:

> Philosophy makes no secret of it. The confession of Prometheus, "In a word I hate all the gods," is its own confession, its own verdict against all gods heavenly and earthly who do not acknowledge human self-consciousness as the supreme deity.[3]

More than simple disbelief, Marx's atheism must be described as a Promethean hatred of anything that claimed or was claimed to stand superior to man and so to constrain or limit man. It was an attitude, or a passion, as defiant of the Greek conception of a divinely instituted order of the world fatal to trespass against (*Moira*) as of the Judeo-Christian God. As its corollary in his dissertation Marx laid down a proposition that would later gain support from Darwin's notion of an indefinitely continuing evolution and that might be called the fundamental creed of the Left: everything, Marx unqualifiedly asserted, could be different from what it was.[4] In effect Marx said, and said belligerently, that man could and should assume powers once regarded as God's.

Barred by that and by similar affronts to Prussian orthodoxy from a hoped-for university post as a lecturer in philosophy, Marx turned to journalism. There his energy and learning quickly brought him the editorship of a radical Rhineland newspaper. In that capacity he was drawn into controversies over local economic concerns, whereupon, through voracious reading, he bagan to add economics to his intellectual armament. Prussian censors, however, soon suppressed his newspaper, and in 1843 Marx moved to Paris for close study of socialism among the expatriate socialists and communists concentrated there. In Paris Marx met and began his lifelong association with Friedrich Engels, whose socialist writings on economics had already gained Marx's warm approval.

As the above suggests, Marx's attention to the impact of economics on politics and history was by no means as unprecedented as his admirers sometimes make out. The 18th and 19th centuries had produced a veritable explosion of writing on "political economy," and Marx laid such socialist economists as Saint-Simon, Sismondi, and Proud'hon, and such non-socialists as Adam Smith and David Ricardo, under heavy contribution. Nor was Marx at all unique in humanitarian concern for industrial wageworkers. During Marx's lifetime not only did Lassalle in Germany but Louis Napoleon in France and Disraeli in England make those workers' often hideous plight a foremost political issue.

More pertinent to our concern with Marx's sociology and theory of history, in Paris Marx aimed at his former mentor Hegel's philosophy a book entitled *Critique of Hegel's Philosophy of Right*. Only the Introduction of Marx's book was published in his lifetime, but that Introduction brilliantly illuminated the intimate connection between Marx's atheism and his deepening political radicalism. Marx wrote:

This society, this state, produce religion . . . . The struggle
against religion is, therefore, indirectly a struggle against the
world whose spiritual aroma is religion.

Religion is the sigh of the oppressed creature . . . . It is the
opium of the people.

Thus the criticism of heaven is transformed into the
criticism of earth, the criticism of religion into the criticism of
law, and the criticism of theology into the criticism of politics.'

Chiefly inspiring Marx's *Critique* and leading him
signally to alter his commitment to Hegel, was Feuerbach's
just-published *Preliminary Theses on the Reform of Philosophy*.
Some alteration of Marx's commitment to Hegel had
already occurred. Where Hegel had envisioned a Spirit
whose essence was freedom realizing itself especially in his
native Prussia and England, recent allies against Napoleon,
Marx, harried for his radicalism by Prussian censors, had
become a man without a country, an ardent inter-
nationalist. Feuerbach's new book, however, prompted a
larger alteration.

Philosophy, Feuerbach asserted, should begin not with
an Idea or Spirit (which Hegel sometimes called God) but
with the observable realities of the actual world. That em-
piricist dictum at once appealed to Marx, and in his *Critique*
we find him rejecting Hegel's conception of an Idea or
Spirit realizing itself in historical reality. For Marx, history
now becomes the record of empirical man realizing or, it
might be said, increasingly humanizing himself in and
through his economic or, as Marx calls it, "material" activity. And where Hegel had found Spirit realizing itself
through ever higher syntheses of opposing philosophies,
Marx, while continuing to conceive history Hegel-wise as a
progressive development that proceeded dialectically, i.e.,
through clashes of opposing forces, finds these forces not in
ideas but in economic classes whose conflict would be

resolved and end in communist society. With this "materialism," which he might better have called economism, Marx came to feel that he had turned Hegel's dialectical philosophy "right side up." He soon concluded that in economic or "material" life and in the class antagonisms to which it gave rise he had identified history's effective causes.

Accordingly, in his *Critique* Marx inverts Hegel's presupposition that states and constitutions determine the way of life of peoples subject to them. In Marx's view, ways of life, at bottom economic life, determine state forms and constitutions, which only ratify and protect economic orders. And Marx goes on in a "criticism of politics" to develop the conviction that in still-feudal Germany no mere constitutional reform can free the nation from princely rule. Asserting that only the total overthrow of the existing order can achieve a real emancipation, Marx declares that only proletarians are earnest and daring enough to tackle that job. Disdaining a socialism that ineffectually draws up blueprints for a better and juster world, Marx urges radical political action. Thus, in his 25th year, in his long-unpublished critique of Hegel's philosophy, Marx sets a course from which neither age nor experience would cause him to deviate.

At this same time in Paris, in manuscripts brought to light only in the 1930's and known as his Paris Manuscripts of 1844, Marx reviewed and probed for its full meaning nearly the whole range of his burgeoning economic, political, and philosophical perceptions. Disjointed, frequently elliptical, written only for himself, these manuscripts assemble most of the structural members of the comprehensive socio-historical doctrine whose expression in the *Communist Manifesto* and *Capital* eventually gained the world's attention.

Seeking the logical consequences of an unbridled capitalist pursuit of profit, Marx in his Paris Manuscripts finds it to be, beyond wageworkers' impoverishment, the same workers' "alienation," which in Marx's usage means more than disaffection or a state of mind. Alienation occurs when men's own creations, especially their means of production or social structures, turn against them and stunt or suppress, and thereby estrange them from, their very humanity. Marx sees these conditions of labor in capitalist industry effecting this estrangement, and in urging a communist alternative he exhibits much of the thinking on which, along with his exaltation of man as "the supreme deity," his admirers base their assertion of his essential humanism.

Marx disdains as mere "crude communism" any program aiming at no more than the overthrow of capitalists and re-distribution of wealth.⁶ Such communism, Marx writes, would only universalize private property and the cupidity it fosters. He warns that it might produce a society even more basely materialistic (in the usual sense of that word) than the capitalist society it displaced. His own larger and higher-minded vision of communism derives from philosophical reflection on the all-engulfing industrialization that in his day was transforming Europe and America.

Not only in Marx's view were the owners of multiplying mines and factories turning peasants and small farmers who had once possessed rights to land into helpless proletarians; not only were they making cupidity a way of life; they were ensnaring the entire human race in a worldwide system of industry and commerce that was coming to govern man instead of being governed by him. As Feuerbach in his *Essence of Christianity* had seen men bowing down before a God who was only a projection of man himself, so Marx saw a human race to whose potential he perceived no limit intolerably constrained and stultified, and thereby alienated from its rightful majesty, by an industrial system that men themselves had created.

In that perception Marx differed little from his future revolutionary rival, the anarchist Mikhail Bakunin. But, where Bakunin came to urge wholesale destruction of the industrial system, Marx in 1844 and to the end of his life wholeheartedly believed that, despite its existing evils, modern industry had "prepared the emancipation of mankind." In agreement with enthusiasts for technological-industrial development in our day, capitalist and socialist alike, Marx saw in modern industry a power that in the right hands could vault mankind into a promised land of freedom, peace, and plenty. Freed from the incubus of private ownership, modern industry could be made the economic base of a "realm of freedom" in which "the complete realization of all human senses and qualities," the complete realization of man's potential, would occur. This communism, which in Marx's usage was coming to denote both a desired type of society and the philosophy that announced that society's coming, presented itself not only as "fully developed naturalism," as atheism and humanism both, but also as "the solution to the riddle of history."

Admitting that man could not claim to be wholly and rightfully his own master if he owed his existence to something other than himself, Marx in his Paris Manuscripts addresses the question that, fifteen years later, Darwin's selection theory would appear to answer. As posed by Marx, this is the question of the origin or cause of the first man. And here communism's and naturalism's masterbuilder finds himself at a loss. He admits to a hypothetical questioner that the notion that man does not owe his existence to something other than himself contradicts normal intelligence. It clashes, he writes, with "everything tangible in practical life." Yet to Marx the clear dependency and contingency of man's existence seems intolerable. Marx ends by simply forbidding his original question. He darkly writes:

> . . . for socialist man the whole of what is called world history is nothing but the creation of man by human labor . . . . [Man] therefore has the evident and irrefutable proof of his own self-creation . . . .[7]

Early in 1845 Marx's involvement with the journal that had printed the Introduction to his critique of Hegel's philosophy resulted in his expulsion from France and removal to Brussels. There in notebook sentences known as his Theses on Feuerbach, sentences whose formal numbering on notebook pages indicates his sense of their finality and importance, Marx carries further the concern for practice or action that had surfaced in his critique of Hegel. In these theses he makes practical, above all political, action the source and judge of truth.

"The question," Marx writes, "whether objective truth can be achieved by human thinking . . . is a practical question. Man must prove the truth . . . of his thinking in practice." While applauding Feuerbach's assertion of religion's purely human origin, he declares even Feuerbach's philosophy insufficient to overcome religion and clear the way for communism. Men, Marx writes, in a derogation of human mind and reason stronger than Darwin's "horrid doubt" of it, are products of circumstances; men think as circumstances compel them to think.

For Marx this means that communist philosophy must be proved true not by appeals to fact and reason but by action that creates the circumstances in which that philosophy will gain acceptance as truth. Thus truth appears to be what men, or Marx, by might and main, can make it. Philosophers, Marx concludes his Theses, have tried only to interpret, i.e., to understand, the world; "the point, however, is to change it."[8]

In the spring of 1845 Engels joined Marx in Brussels, where they began work together on *The German Ideology*, another book that saw publication only after Marx's death. While the book devotes most of its considerable length to criticisms of its authors' former mentors and allies, its first chapter contains the nearest to a general statement of Marx's central doctrine that Marx ever offered.

In its first pages *The German Ideology* peremptorily lays down what can be called an anthropological foundation for Marx's "materialist" assertion of the overriding causal power of economic policy and practice. Man, we read, is distinguished from other animals not by speech or rational thought, not by religion or morality, nor by lust for power, but by his production of his means of subsistence. In that activity Marx and Engels discover man's essential nature. For them, man is essentially a producer of economic goods; economic production specifies the human race.[9]

That foundation laid, *The German Ideology* presents an overview of history and social change that begins with tribal society and continues through ancient and feudal societies to the society marked by private ownership of the means of production. Neither philosophical thought nor religion, neither national nor dynastic rivalries, nor politics in any narrow sense, constitute the matter of this overview.

Marx and Engels focus instead on economic life. Their interest centers on the increasing division of labor occasioned by man's historically improving means of production and on the conflicts which that division successively creates. Conflict emerges between townsmen and rural agriculturalists, divides commercial and industrial interests, and climaxes between capitalist owners of the means of production and proletarians forced by modern mass production into, as Marx sees it, numbingly trivial, hence alienating, specialization.

Repeating one of the leading ideas of Marx's critique of Hegel's philosophy, *The German Ideology* perceives social structures and political constitutions continually changing in response to economic change. It points to revolutionary upset of successive orders and elites as "the driving force of history, also of religion, of philosophy and all other kinds of theory." Though Marx seems to have expected communist society, once installed, to endure forever, a commentator charitably inclined can derive from *The German Ideology* and Marx's later writings an undoubtedly sound perception of the historicity and hence impermanence of every social and economic order. Certainly, *The German Ideology* portrays capitalism not as an order finally settled upon and fixed in the nature of things, as bourgeois economists tended to portray it, but as a phase or configuration of still-continuing history and therefore open to thoroughgoing change. There, probably, in his assertion of the impermanence of apparently firmly established social structures, is Marx's most convincing contribution to social thought—though it should be noted that there Marx, like Darwin in Darwin's denial of special creation, only varied a theme that had been more than familiar to the Doctors of the Church. As

Augustine had put it in *The City of God*, states, empires, and all human contrivance "totter through the one transitory instability."

Rejecting as "utopian" all socialist proposals depending for their realization on men's good will, *The German Ideology* finds the historical conditions for communist revolution already present and premonitory. These conditions appear in capitalists' creation of an enormously productive industry and a growing proletariat, the latter a class so deprived that it "no longer counts as a class," one whose revolt and triumph will at last end class conflict and install a classless communist society. And that society, Marx and Engels declare, will somehow—they furnish no particulars—eliminate the dehumanizing specialization of labor imposed by capitalist-owned industry.[10] Under communism, previously stunted, alienated proletarians will become whole, all-around men; communism will prove the road to the full humanization of man whose prophet and champion Marx felt himself to be.

To Marx's prediction of proletarian revolution and a high-minded communist future the objection might at once arise that a proletarian revolution would at best install the crude communism that Marx had earlier disdained. As if aware of that objection, Marx and Engels answer it with a conception that Marx frequently repeated later, especially in his attack on the gradualism of the Social Democrats' Gotha Program and in the last volume of *Capital*: out of the revolutionary violence that the overthrow of capitalism would require, out of a purgatory of class war and terror, a *new man* would emerge. Purified and ennobled by revolutionary action, that new man would be, as Trotsky later described him, "a higher social-biological type, if you will, a superman." In *The German Ideology* Marx and Engels phrased this remarkable conception, to which Darwin's assertion of man's continuing evolution soon brought support, this way:

> Both for the production on a mass scale of communist consciousness, and for the success of the cause itself, the alteration of men on a mass scale is necessary, an alteration which can only take place in a practical movement, a revolution; the revolution is necessary, therefore, not only because the ruling class cannot be overthrown in any other way, but also because the class overthrowing it can only in a revolution succeed in ridding itself of the muck of ages and become fitted to found society anew.[11]

That class war and revolution, "the brutal contradiction, body against body," as Marx put it a year later in *The Poverty of Philosophy*, seem of all things the least likely to engender the altruistic wisdom required for a society free of cupidity and class antagonism seems not to have occurred to Marx. In any event his dependence on the notion that they would engender it posed another pressing problem: would the transfiguring revolution ever actually take place, would a truly communist society ever be more than a cherished dream?

Marx and Engels answered Yes, and in the *Communist Manifesto* of 1848 they added to the ideas already described another and, for completed Marxism, necessary one. This was the idea, adumbrated in Marx's Paris Manuscripts, that capitalism's own dynamic or, as Marx put it years later in *Capital*, "the natural laws of capitalist production . . . working with iron necessity toward inevitable results," guaranteed the revolution's coming.[12] Capitalism would so immiserate the proletariat that the revolution must erupt.

Though coinciding in 1848 with the outbreak of socialist and other insurgencies all over Europe, the

Manifesto was not a call to arms. Commissioned by an international Communist League newly come into the open, an organization of which Marx and Engels were leading members, the *Manifesto* aimed instead to *prepare* the revolution by educating and uniting proletarians in all countries. Claiming by virtue of their "materialism" a profound insight into history, Marx and Engels offered a vigorous account of Europe's transition from feudalism to capitalism. With this account they sought to convince socialists prone to compromises and ineffective theorizing that history was on their side, that the momentum of the ages would vindicate and actualize socialists' most radical and far-reaching hopes. On this appeal to history and their understanding of it Marx and Engels based their lifelong contention that their socialism, unlike socialism dependent on men's good will, was scientific.

Marx took the lead in composing the *Manifesto*, and here, at considerable length, he speaks for himself:

> From the serfs of the Middle Ages sprang the chartered burghers of the earliest towns. From these burgesses the first elements of the bourgeoisie were developed. The discovery of America, the rounding of the Cape, opened up fresh ground for the rising bourgeoisie . . . . The feudal system of industry, in which industrial production was monopolized by closed guilds, now no longer sufficed . . . . The guildmasters were pushed aside by the manufacturing middle class . . . . Meanwhile the markets kept ever growing, the demand ever rising . . . . Thereupon steam and machinery revolutionized industrial production. The place of [cottage] manufacture was taken by the giant, Modern Industry, the place of the industrial middle class by industrial millionaires . . . .
>
> We see then: the means of production and of exchange on whose foundation the bourgeoisie built itself up, were generated in feudal society. At a certain stage in the development of those means of production and exchange . . . the feudal

relations of property became no longer compatible with the already developed productive force; they became so many fetters. They had to be burst asunder; they were burst asunder.

A similar movement is going on before our eyes . . . . But not only has the bouregeoisie forged the weapons [steam and machinery] that bring death to itself; it has also called into being the men who are to wield those weapons . . . the proletarians . . . . Owing to the extensive use of machinery and division of labor, the work of the proletarians has lost all individual character and, consequently, all charm for the workman. He becomes an appendage of the machine, and it is only the most simple, the most monotonous, and most easily acquired knack that is required of him. . . . In proportion, therefore, as the repulsiveness of the work increases, the wage decreases.

And here it becomes evident that the bourgeoisie is unfit any longer to be the ruling class . . . . It is unfit to rule because it is incompetent to assure an existence to its slave within his slavery, because it cannot help letting him sink into such a state that it has to feed him instead of being fed by him . . . . What the bourgeoisie therefore produces, above all, are its own gravediggers. Its fall and the victory of the proletariat are alike inevitable.

In place of the old bourgeois society . . . we shall have an association [of the people] in which the free development of each is the condition of the free development of all.

[Communists] openly declare that their ends can be obtained only by the forcible overthrow of all existing social conditions . . . . Working men of all countries, unite!$^{\prime\prime}$

A few years later in a letter to a correspondent Marx staked out his claim to originality in these words:

As far as I am concerned, I cannot claim to have discovered the existence of classes in modern society or their strife against one another. Petty bourgeois historians long ago described the evolution of class struggles, and the political economists showed the economic physiology of the classes. I have added as a new contribution the following propositions: (1) that the existence of classes is bound up with certain phases of material production, (2) that the class struggle leads necessarily to the dictatorship of the proletariat, (3) that this dictatorship is but the transition to the abolition of all classes and to the creation of a society of the free and equal. [14]

By the time the *Manifesto* had appeared in print, the revolutionary tide of 1848 was threatening Belgium, and the Belgian government ordered Marx to leave. Welcomed in Paris by a newly organized Provisional Government, he stayed there until unrest and rioting broke out in Germany, whereupon he moved to Cologne and sought to fan the revolutionary fire with radical journalism. German governments, however, rode out the storm, and a (bourgeois) jury acquitted Marx of a charge of treason. In 1849 Marx went to London. For a year or more he expected revolution to break out again on the Continent and call him back, but his stay in London proved permanent.

In London Marx plunged into a prolonged and never quite concluded grapple with economic theory. Over the years this resulted in his *Critique of Political Economy* of 1859 and in the re-working of that book's economic content in *Capital*, whose last two volumes were composed by Engels from Marx's notes. Though *Capital* foresees that control of industry will pass from founding entrepreneurs to professional managers and technicians, and though it claims that communists will use modern industry's productivity to shorten working hours, it does not significantly modify the thrust and meaning of Marx's earlier writings. It mainly attempts to ground in a theory of "surplus value," itself grounded in classical economists' now-discredited labor theory of value, the *Manifesto*'s declaration that capitalism must inevitably issue in proletarian misery and revolution. [15] Marx's writings during his London years added little to the panoramic socio-historical doctrine he had constructed earlier.

Marx never set down a complete general statement of his doctrine. Instead he expounded it piecemeal and, as in the *Manifesto*'s account of the rise of capitalism from feudal beginnings, offered examples of it in discussion of particular issues. In consequence some Marxists tell us that in Marxism we have not a theory of history and society open to criticism as such but only a "mode of critical thought." In fact, not only the writings we have referred to but many others in the Marxian canon abound in lapidary statements about history and society, not merely about how to think about them. A theory of history, claiming validity from man's "self-creation" through the present to the future, tacitly supports Marx's particular statements and makes them comprehensible. Commonly called historical materialism and as such given respectful attention by his apologists, it is also sometimes called the economic interpretation of history.

That last locution, however, may suggest what Marx never intended and what no sort or sect of Marxists takes seriously, namely that Marx's is only one interpretation of history and that others are admissible. Marx advanced his interpretation as the only true one, and it is the only one that his admirers find worthy of discussion. It follows with fair coherence from his specification of man as a self-created producer of his means of subsistence. We can summarize it this way:

The means of production, i.e., the implements and techniques of production, in use at any period require for their maximum exploitation a particular social structure. Because man is foremost and essentially a producer of his means of subsistence, maximum exploitation occurs and the required social structure arises. At the same time a superstructure of political and legal institutions, morality, and religion also arises to protect and sanctify the social structure. Thus, as Marx put it in his Paris Manuscripts, "religion, the family, the state, law, morality, science, art, etc., are only particular forms of production." The whole edifice then endures without serious challenge until more efficient means of production appear. The existing social structure cramps and fetters these new means, preventing their full exploitation, whereupon, with general popular support, the community or class possessing them overthrows the social structure and its spiritual superstructure and makes itself pre-eminent. With that, a new social structure and spiritual superstructure arise. Thus history has been a series of social revolutions triggered by improvements of the means of production.

Our summary continues:

With the rise of modern industry and private ownership of the means of production, those means and the social structure have once more come into conflict or "contradiction." Capitalist industry has so magnified production that it can abundantly satisfy all men's economic needs, yet by lowering wages capitalism so impoverishes the proletarians who could be its customers and on whose labor it depends that the means of production are not fully exploited and proletarians' very survival is threatened. Moreover, by concentrating wealth in fewer and fewer hands—"one capitalist kills many," we read in *Capital*'s first volume—capitalism is eliminating small capitalists and independent tradesmen and thereby preparing an unmediated class conflict that will be more violent than any in the past. The outcome is inevitable: increasing numbers of desperate proletarians will overthrow capitalist society and install a "dictatorship of the proletariat" in which class distinctions vanish. Having brought under its control an economic system that threatened to control *it*, a mankind transfigured by revolutionary action will move through socialism, which rewards individuals according to their social contribution, to a purely voluntary communism based on the rule of "from each according to his ability, to each according to his need."[16] Thus the economic system will become the necessary economic base of a "realm of freedom" in which man achieves full humanity.

As Darwin made a struggle for existence decided by natural selection the prime mover of a biological process moving toward biological perfection, so Marx made economic effort the prime mover of an historical process moving toward social perfection.

Given the prominence of economic effort in any struggle for existence, Lenin did not go far wrong, if wrong at all, when he wrote, "The whole theory of Marx is an application of the [Darwin's] theory of evolution—in its most consistent, well-thought-out, and fruitful form . . . ."[17] In 1869 Marx himself wrote to Engels that Darwin's *Origin of Species* provided "the basis in natural history for our views."

In the previous chapter we remarked the essential ferocity of Darwin's selection theory of evolution. That ferocity, too, has its parallel in Marxism. Rather more evidence exists for it than Marxist educators commonly tell their students. By "revolution" Marx meant forcible, i.e., violent and bloody, revolution. On that point there is little room for doubt. Marx did assert that revolution's futility if it were launched before its time had come; the conditions for success had to ripen "in the womb of the old society itself." But once those conditions had ripened, once the decisive hour had struck, Marx prescribed terror, bloodletting, and, too often overlooked in academia today, attack on democratically-minded allies, whom his apostle Lenin succinctly called "useful idiots." Marx made much of this

explicit in composing the Address of the Central Commit-
tee to the Communist League in 1850. There he wrote:

> Above all things, the workers must counteract, as much as
> it is possible during the conflict and immediately after the
> struggle, the petty bourgeois endeavors to allay the storm, and
> must compel the democrats to carry out their terrorist words . .
> . . Far from opposing so-called excesses, instances of popular
> revenge against hated individuals . . . must not only be
> tolerated but the leadership of them must be taken in hand . . . .
> [From] the first moment of victory mistrust must be directed
> not against the conquered reactionary party, but against the
> workers' previous allies . . . . [18]

In 1850 also, Marx allied himself with the notorious
French terrorist Blanqui. Two years later Marx's *Eighteenth
Brumaire of Louis Napoleon* re-emphasized his disdain of
democracy. In 1870 Marx attributed the defeat of the Paris
Commune of that year, an uprising he had once called
premature, to its leaders' lack of sufficient revolutionary
vengefulness. In 1875 the Social Democrats' Gotha
Program drew his fire not only for its gradualism but also
for its "ideological nonsense about 'right' and other trash
among the democrats."[19]

In such pronouncements we see the basis of the
strategy uniformly employed by Marxist revolutionaries. In
the Russian, Chinese, Cuban, Vietnamese, Zimbabwean,
Nicaraguan and other revolutions that strategy has unfolded in three successive steps: (1) gain political power
with the help of democratic "useful idiots"; (2) eliminate
the "useful idiots"; (3) establish a dictatorship.

*   *   *

The mind-relaxing comprehensiveness of Marx's
doctrine, coupled with a promise of harmony and plenty

delivered by an apparently hard-headed student of social realities, has carried many an uncritical mind along to warm agreement. To critical minds, however, the objections to it seem as numerous as they are overwhelming. Only the following will be mentioned here:

Man's "self-creation" is simply unintelligible. Man owes his being to causes other than himself—and this powerfully suggests that the same or equally unknown causes will do much to shape his future.

That man's production of his means of subsistence suffices to specify him cannot be believed on the strength of Marx's bald assertion.

We remarked earlier that in workers' increasing wages and in the outcomes of Marxist revolutions 20th-century events have taken decidedly un-Marxian turns. Here we note that not "the laws of capitalist production" but small cadres of revolutionists in largely pre-capitalist countries have accomplished Marxist revolutions. Following their success, the "higher social-biological type" that Marx persuaded his followers to expect has failed to appear. Biologically speaking, as we saw in discussion of Darwinism, man was as fully human a hundred thousand years ago as he seems likely ever to become. Psychosocially speaking, no seasoned mind will expect class war and revolution to improve man's moral nature. The notion that class war and revolution would produce a new and morally exemplary man lies at the core of Marxism, and must be called absurd.

To whatever extent the industrial system has been made the base of a realm of freedom it has been made such in the non-Marxist West. Thanks to voters and politicians, to such writers as Victor Hugo, Carlyle, Charles Dickens, and J. S. Mill, to early union organizers, to workers themselves, and to not a few capitalists, all of whose efforts Marx scorned, a huge amelioration of workers' condition occurred during Marx's lifetime and for generations afterward—without the revolutionary violence Marx called for and promoted. The good will shrugged off by Marx in favor of his visionary theory of history has not been wholly lacking.

In face of such realities academic Marxists have sometimes viewed Marxism's apocalyptic revolutionary element as mere political rhetoric and sought to prune it from Marxism while retaining Marx's internationalism and "materialist" theory of history. Such pruned Marxism has occasionally found favor also with international business- men and bankers as convinced as Marx of economics' su- preme importance and impatient with national aims and ideals that might restrict business opportunities. But a "materialism" or economism pruned of Marxian prophecy fares little better than Marx's own Marxism when tested against historical fact.

Events in every age have falsified the notion that the cause of social and political change is change in the means of production. All the cataclysmic social, political, and spiritual upheavals involved in the sequence Old Kingdom—Middle Kingdom—New Empire swept over an- cient Egypt, enthroning and dethroning kings and gods, while the Egyptians continued to cultivate the Nile Valley by means inherited from long-dead ancestors. No change in the means of production comes close to accounting for the fall of the Roman Empire and the rise of Christianity, nor, later, for the break-up of medieval Christendom and the rise of nation-states. Nor for the fall of the Weimar Republic and the rise of Hitler. One might go on for pages. One should also mention Max Weber's total reversal of

Marx's "materialism." Weber presented a formidable case for thinking that religious change, specifically Protestantism, accounted for modern industry itself.

Can we not yet call it obvious that in constructing his "materialist" theory of history Marx hugely exaggerated the causal power of economic aims and interests? Change in the means of production simply cannot carry the historical burden Marx placed upon it. Other and perhaps more powerful forces also manifest themselves in history's abundance of wars and creeds, social orders and revolutions, laws, arts, and sciences. The failure of historical materialism to square with historical fact directs attention to the conception of human thought that gives that doctrine its coherence and plausibility. Here we encounter what seems Marx's most enduring legacy.

Marx's conception of human thought bears witness to the influence of the French Enlightenment, whose naturalistic bent Marx pressed to Promethean atheism. Such luminaries of that Enlightenment as Helvetius, Condillac, Holbach, and Lamettrie, the last of whom pronounced man a machine, seem to have sensed in any idea of a free or circumstance-transcending mind more than a trace of the religion that in man's mind had found the image of a transcendent Creator. Enlightenment thought tended in the opposite direction, and Marx, insisting that the "thought process itself is a natural process," followed that direction all the way.

Since the deterministic consequence is profoundly anti-humanist and logically and empirically fallacious, Marx's admirers often try to absolve Marx and Marxism of it. They commonly base this effort on a statement several times made by Marx, that man makes his own history. They ignore Marx's conception of man as a creature specified and motivated by his urge to produce his means of subsistence. The man who in Marx's scheme of things made his own history possessed no more freedom of thought and action than a beaver instinctively building dams or a squirrel instinctively gathering nuts.

In the *German Ideology* of 1846 Marx and Engels wrote:

> In direct opposition to German [Hegelian] philosophy . . . [we] start from actually working people, and from their actual [i.e., economic] life we also present the ideological reflexes and echo of this life process . . . . Morality, religion, metaphysics, and such other ideology and forms of consciousness that correspond to them thus no longer retain the semblance of independence . . . . It is not consciousness that determines life, but life that determines consciousness. [20]

In The Poverty of Philosophy of 1847 Marx again asserted the reflexive, epiphenomenal nature of men's thinking:

> In acquiring new productive forces men change their mode of production; and in changing their mode of production, in changing their way of earning their living, they change all their social relations. The hand-mill gives you society with the feudal lord; the steam-mill, society with the industrial capitalist. The same men who establish their social relations in conformity with their material productivity, produce also principles, ideas, and categories in conformity with their social relations. [21]

In 1848 came the *Manifesto*, in which Marx and Engels asked rhetorically:

> What else does the history of ideas prove, than that intellectual production changes its character in proportion as material production is changed? [22]

A decade later Marx gave his economic determinism its fullest expression in the Preface to his *Critique of Political Economy*:

I was led by my studies to the conclusion that legal relations and the forms of the state could neither be understood by
themselves nor be explained by what was called the general
progress of the human mind, but were rooted in the material
conditions of life . . . . In the social production which men carry
on they enter into definite relations that are indispensable and
independent of their wills . . . . The sum total of these relations
of production constitutes the economic structure of society—
the real foundation, on which rise legal and political
superstructures . . . . The mode of production in material life
determines the general character of the social, political, and
spiritual processes of life. It is not the consciousness of men
that determines their existence, but, on the contrary, their
social existence determines their consciousness.[23]

In full maturity Marx re-asserted the same conception
in his Preface to the 1873 edition of *Capital*'s first volume:

—for Hegel the thought-process . . . is the demiurge of the real,
which is only its external garment. With me, on the contrary,
the ideal [thought] is nothing but the material transformed
and transplanted in the head of man.

Finally, to make an end, Engels's Preface to the 1888
English edition of the *Manifesto* advises:

The *Manifesto* being our joint production, I consider myself
bound to state that the fundamental proposition which forms
its nucleus belongs to Marx. That proposition is: that in every
historical epoch, the prevailing mode of economic production
and exchange, and the social organization necessarily following from it, form the basis upon which is built up, and from
which alone can be explained, the political and intellectual
history of the epoch.[24]

That "materialist" conception of thought denies the
existence of anything properly called mind. It substitutes
for mind an irrational, involuntary reflection of economic
interest that produces only an epiphenomenal "ideology."

There we discover not only the nucleus of the *Manifesto* but the nucleus and binding cement of Marx's whole socio-historical doctrine. Where Darwin had more or less unwittingly made men's thinking a reflex of the struggle for survival, Marx wittingly and repeatedly made men's thinking a reflex of economic interest. Having delivered that irrationalist assertion early in his career, Marx thereafter lost few opportunities to exhibit scorn for ideas in general— except his own. In his later years he pressed a polemic against "ideological reflexes and echoes" and "philosophical phantasmagoria" that has found lasting echo in modern sophistication.

Where Darwin implicitly denied the existence of free or self-determining mind, Marx denied it explicitly. And that explicit denial, like Darwin's implicit one, incorporates a rebound against itself, a self-cancellation, that makes Marx's own thought as irrational or involuntary as any capitalist's or untaught proletarian's. If thought only rationalizes economic or class interest, must not Marx's do the same?[25] Of course it must. In all logic, Marx placed truth or objectivity beyond the reach of any human.

"So much for logic!" the reply may come from Marxist catechumens viewing logic as a bourgeois pseudo-science. "Was Marx right or wrong about man's thinking?"

Marx was wrong. His mind-denying conception of human thought as a reflex of the mode of production or of class interest stands in blatant contradiction to obvious realities:

First, ideas in individual human heads always precede their objectification in means of production or in societies or classes conscious of themselves as such. Henry Ford thought of the assembly line before he built it, and Marx labored all his life to implant his own ideas in proletarians to make them a community conscious of itself as such. An idea comes first; the inluence of its objectification comes later.

Second, men in historical periods marked by hugely different modes of production often share the same ideas; though often under other names Platonists and Sophists exist today as they did in ancient Greece. Likewise, men in different classes often share the same ideas, while men in the same class often differ fundamentally. Still other men change their ideas without changing their class or, perforce, the period in which they live. Ideas do not simply reflect historical periods' means of production or individuals' class membership. Contradictions of that supposed rule meet us everywhere. Under scrutiny, Marx's irrationalist conception of human thought dissolves. Quite obvious considerations reveal, at the heart of a doctrine that in tirelessly revised interpretations gained a tight hold on countless intellectuals, an astonishing indifference not only to logic but to the plainest sort of fact.

Marx died before the above objections made sufficient noise to require a public answer. The burden of answering them fell on Engels, who accepted it in the 1890's. In a series of letters published in German journals favorable to Marxism Engels laid down the line followed ever since by Marx's apologists.

Marx, Engels wrote, had been crudely misunderstood. Engels granted that both he and Marx might have been "partly [sic] responsible for the fact that the younger men have sometimes laid more stress on the economic side than it deserves." Actually, he went on, "Marx never meant to claim an absolute validity for economic considerations to the exclusion of all other factors"[26]—and it is true that Marx in his much-quoted statement, "I, at least, am not a

Marxist" and in one or two private letters toward the end of his life alleged the same.

Good for Marx, one comments. But at the same time one asks why, if Marx had not meant what he said, he had said it so emphatically and so often. Or why Engels himself had said it independently in his Anti-Dühring articles in the 1870's. There Engels had written:

> —the final causes of all social changes and political revolutions arc to be sought, not in men's brains . . . but in changes in the mode of production and exchange. They are to be sought, not in the *philosophy*, but in the *economics* of each particular period.[27] (Emphases Engels's)

The answer to the question above is plain. Marx and Engels so emphatically and so often asserted a thoroughgoing economic determinism because their whole conception of society and history turned upon it. Without it, the whole Marxian construction collapses. Economic determinism absent, social structures and spiritual superstructures would not, as in fact they do not, rise and fall in response to changes in the means of production. Economic determinism absent, rational discussion and debate might achieve some part of the good that Marx declared only revolution could achieve. Economic determinism distinguishes and specifies Marx's and Engels's sociology.

As we have seen Marx writing, bourgeois historians had earlier described "the evolution of class struggles." Political economists had "showed the economic physiology of the classes." Nor was it news that economic interest sometimes overrode all else and governed individuals' thought and action. That last truth receives strong emphasis in the Bible. But Hebrew prophets, Christian Fathers, and scientists from Thales to Newton had often explicitly said and always predicated their activity upon the

belief that men could, with discipline and effort, overcome
the pull of circumstance and personal interest. Historical
materialism, Marxism, asserted that that belief was false,
that ideas and ideals possessed "no semblance of independence" and were only "the material [the economic]
transformed and translated in the head of man."

Where human thought came into question nothing
else remained for Marx to say. Any weaker statement had
been made before—and no weaker statement could sustain
his theory of society and history. His theory required the
unqualified statements he so often made. That economic affairs not only affected or conditioned history but actually
determined it was and is the distinguishing mark of Marxism. Admit that political, philosophical, and other ideas do
not merely reflect economics, grant those ideas an origin
and causal power of their own, and you have made a
withdrawal of Marx's doctrine as comprehensive in its effect as the withdrawal of Darwin's doctrine in Darwin's
final appeal to unknown causes.

That Engels in denying that Marx had claimed absolute validity for economic considerations appeared to
have made such a withdrawal was quickly recognized by E.
R. A. Seligman, an avowed Marxist occupying Columbia
University's chair of political science. In 1907 Seligman
acknowledged in his *Economic Interpretation of History*:

> —when we read the latest exposition of their views by one of
> the founders themselves, it almost seems as if the whole theory
> of economic interpretation had been thrown overboard . . . .

Seligman then added:

> It would be a mistake, however, to suppose that these conces-
> sions, undeniably significant as they are, involved in the minds
> of the leaders an abandonment of the theory . . . .

Focussing on the minds of the leaders, Seligman went on to quote Engels's sequel to his disavowal of the economic determinism that he and Marx had so often affirmed. Attempting to rescue what unanswerable objections had forced him publicly, and Marx privately, to back away from, Engels had written:

> It is not that the economic situation is the cause, in the sense of being the only active agent, while all [other] phenomena are only a passive result. It is, on the contrary, a case of mutual action on the basis of mutual necessity, which in the last instance always works itself out.

Are those words not hopelessly equivocal? If mutual action between economic and other aims and interests occurs, those other aims and interests affect thought and history as much as economic ones and may, as they often do, move us in un-economic directions. Which contradicts historical materialism. While if all things happen on the basis of an economic necessity that in the last instance always works itself out, there can be no truly mutual action. Marx and Engels cannot have it both ways.

In various phrasings the same equivocal effort to absolve Marx and themselves of a determinism that denies the integrity of all thought, including their own thought, comes again and again from Marx's apologists and epigones. The American socialist Michael Harrington furnishes a recent example. He posits an "organic merger" of economic and mental forces that creates an "atmosphere" that "bathes" all decisions and somehow allows economic forces to work themselves out without actually determining human thought. Such verbal writhing betrays the centrality of economic determinism to Marxist doctrine.

Other Marxists hasten plainly to reject Marx's determinism, but in the next moment assert conclusions that re-

quire it if they are to make any sense at all.[28] Marxists subjected to criticism have been well compared to pillows that
yield easily to pressure but resume their original shape
when the pressure is lifted.

In sum, for intellectual decency's sake Marx's determinism must be disavowed, but it cannot be disavowed
without collapsing Marxism.

In truth, as most of us know, interaction between
men's minds and economic and other circumstance un-
ceasingly goes on. The crucial question is whether minds
interact with circumstances that minds have in part
produced and can affect—or whether minds interact with
circumstances that formed minds in the first place and
determine them.

To that crucial question Marx's atheism impelled him
to give a mistaken and thoroughly anti-humanist answer.
Carrying with it the conception of human thought as a
purely natural process, his atheism meant that thought
could have "no semblance of independence" and had to be
accounted for by circumstance. Beyond its rank derogation
of man's mind, that answer generates the absurd idea that
human creations, say the U.S. Constitution or Mozart's
music, are transmitted to their authors by circumstances or
environments in which those creations do not exist. To
avoid that absurdity, some measure of freedom and
creativity must be attributed to human minds.

Marx perceived and pilloried the stark inhumanity
that all too often characterized early modern industry. But
in so doing he was by no means unique and very far from
being the most effective. Nor, with his conception of man as
a creature driven only by economic need and interest, could
he conceive of any humane or realistic correction of that inhumanity. In consequence he placed his hope and per-

suaded others to place their hope in revolutionary violence and a "dictatorship of the proletariat." That the dictatorship proved one of revolutionaries only, and that it ended in the self-perpetuating dictatorships of Lenin, Stalin, and their successors and parallels in other countries seems owing not to any betrayal of Marx. Though occurring in vastly different European, oriental, and African societies, Marxist revolutions have without exception ended in one-party or one-man tyrannies. At fault is the basic unrealism and irrationalism of Marxist doctrine. At fault in the "useful idiots" who still excuse and close their eyes to Marxism's actual results is an overweening confidence in their own good intentions. Many pages back, the reader may have wondered why a son of well-to-do, responsible parents should in his sheltered student life have developed a hatred of religion that Marx displayed. One must not attach too much weight to youthful versifying, but the following lines written by Marx during his first year at Berlin do seem pertinent):

> With disdain I throw my gauntlet
> Full in the face of the world
>
> *   *   *
>
>
> *   *   *
>
> Then will I wander godlike and victorious
> Through the ruins of the world
> And, giving my words an active force,
> I will feel equal to the Creator.[29]

What moved Marx to want to change the world rather than understand it, to substitute communist agitation for philosophy, and to declare man self-created may have been envy of his Creator.

The Polish refugee Lesjek Kolakowski wrote recently that Marx had promoted a vision of the future whose realization could be attempted only by a despotism that violated the same vision. Kolakowski went on to remark "the strange fate of an idea that began in Promethean humanism and culminated in the monstrous tyranny of Stalin." Actually, that fate seems a good deal less than strange. For Marx's humanism will seem humane only to those who share it. To Jews and Christians it will seem demonic. To such Greeks as Aeschylus Promethean humanism seemed sheer madness. It drove Karl Marx, a learned and far from stupid man, into conflict with the plainest sort of fact, into fostering political regimes that he himself would probably have despised, and into an irrationalism and denial of the freedom of man's mind whose cost in war, tyranny, and despair continues every year to mount.

Notes on Chapter II

1. Merton, *On Theoretical Sociology,* 1949, p. 161, *passim.*

2. Bell, *The Coming of Post-Industrial Society,* 1973, p. 40.

3. Eric Voegelin's translation in his *Science, Politics, and Gnosticism,* 1968, p. 35.

4. H. P. Adams, *Karl Marx in His Earlier Writings,* 1940, p. 37.

5. Marx's Introduction to his *A Contribution to the Critique of Hegel's Philosophy of Right* in *Karl Marx, Early Writings,* trans. and ed. T. B. Bottomore, 1964.

6. Ibid., p. 153.

7. Ibid., p. 139.

8. Marx-Engels: Collected Works, Lawrence and Wishart, London, 1976, vol. V, pp. 3-5.

9. Ibid., vol. V, p. 290.

10. Marx and Engels, *The German Ideology,* trans. and ed. Progress Publishers, Moscow, 1976, p. 53.

11. *Marx-Engels: Collected Works,* Lawrence and Wishart, London, 1976, vol. V (*The German Ideology*), pp. 52-53. Marx repeated the idea in his *Critique of the Gotha Program,* International Publishers ed., 1938, p. 10, and at the end of vol. III of *Capital.*

12. Loc. cit., Author's Preface.

13. Text quoted is that in *The Essential Left: Four Classic Texts*, London, 1960. Present writer has taken some liberties in paragraphing.

14. David McLellan, *Karl Marx, His Life and Thought*, 1973, p. 187n4. Also Karl Marx, *Capital and Other Writings*, Max Eastman, ed., Modern Library, 1932, p. xv.

15. Marx took the labor theory of value—that the labor put into an article correctly measured its value—from such classical economists as Smith and Ricardo. This ran foul of, for example, the value of precious stones and pearls, where labor was minimal. Beginning in Marx's lifetime, Jevons, Walras, Menger, and other economists saw the objection and rejected the theory. Marx's "surplus value" was the difference between the labor put into an article, paid for in subsistence wages, and the price the capitalist received for it. According to this, the more workers a capitalist exploited, the greater was his profit—which ran foul of capitalists' lasting habit of replacing workers with machinery.

16. One is reminded of Augustine's Heavenly City, where "all serve one another in charity." Augustine's City, however, *was* heavenly.

17. Lenin, *The State and Revolution*, in *The Essential Left*, *op. cit.*, p. 222. See also *Karl Marx, Early Writings*, *op. cit.*, p. xiv.

18. Karl Marx, *Selected Works*, Marx-Engels-Lenin Institute ed., Moscow, vol. II, English ed. C. P. Dutt, pp. 163-64.

19. Karl Marx, *Critique of the Gotha Program*, *op. cit.*, p. 10, *passim.*

20. Karl Marx, *Capital and Other Writings*, *op. cit.*, pp. 9-10.

21. Karl Marx, *The Poverty of Philosophy*, vol. XXVI of Marxist Library, International Publishers ed., n.d., p. 92.

22. *The Essential Left*, *op. cit.*, p. 33.

23. Karl Marx, *A Contribution to the Critique of Political Economy*, Charles Kerr and Co. ed., 1904, pp. 11-12.

24. *The Essential Left*, *op. cit.*, p. 12.

25. As even so sympathetic a critic as George Lichtheim observed, Marx simply ignored the dilemma. Cf. Lichtheim, *The Concept of Ideology*, 1967, p. 21.

26. For this and its sequel in the text, see E. R. A. Seligman, *The Economic Interpretation of History*, 1907, pp. 63-64, 148-49. Also Pitirim Sorokin, *Contemporary Sociological Theories*, 1928, p. 533n43.

27. *The Essential Left*, *op. cit.*, p. 126.

28. Here J. K. Galbraith differs from other Marx admirers. In a review of Harrington's *The Twilight of Capitalism* in the *New York Times Book Review*, May 23, 1976, Galbraith wrote: "I have never been able to see why the person who takes Marx's words to mean what they say is always wrong—or naive. Additionally, [Marx's original notion] has always seemed to me a very good description of things as they are."

29. David McLellan, *Karl Marx: His Life and Thought*, *op. cit.*, p. 22.

Chapter III
Freudianism

In Sigmund Freud we encounter a Doctor of modernity whose teaching the celebrated anthropologist Ashley Montagu proclaimed "the most insightful contribution to our understanding of human nature in the history of humanity."[1] In Freud we also encounter the unrivalled Grand Master of qualification, revision, and withdrawal. Freud, it must be said, grew theories as a dog grows hair and shed them as cavalierly. Detailing his sometimes lurid findings in a smooth, unruffled prose that in one edition of his works fills 24 volumes, he repeatedly abandoned theories central to his teaching and replaced them with new ones. That fact has been attested by Professor Calvin S. Hall, who has spread the Freudian illumination at several universities. In the 1950's Hall conscientiously combed through the Freudian canon in an earnest effort to ascertain what in the end Freud really meant to say. Hall's consequent *Primer of Freudian Psychology* advised:

> In the 1920's for example, when Freud was seventy years old, he completely altered a number of his fundamental views. He revamped his theory of motivation, reversed his theory of anxiety, and instituted a new model of personality . . . .[2]

Yet these revisions and reversals were, as Hall re-marked, only examples of Freud's second thought and not, by far, the totality. Others equally significant deserve some mention here.

In his early days, announcing the cure of neuroses via dream interpretation, Freud shrugged off the role of heredity in the formation of neuroses—no one cures heredity—and missed few opportunities to scorn the fine French psycholo-gist, Pierre Janet, who emphasized heredity's importance. In 1932, however, without mentioning Janet, Freud's *New Intro-ductory Lectures* pronounced neuroses "constitutionally deter-mined." Again, though he had begun with the bold an-nouncement that he had freed psychiatry from physiology, the same *New Introductory Lectures* concluded with the expecta-tion that physiology would some day provide psychoanalysis with its "foundation."

A few years earlier Freud had buried in *Civilization and Its Discontents* a withdrawal of the theory on which he had based psychoanalytical therapy and on which Freudian psychoanalysts still base it:

> Neurosis appeared as the outcome of a struggle between the instinct of self-preservation and the claims of the libido, a struggle in which the ego was victorious but at a price of great renunciation and suffering. Every analyst will admit that none of this even now reads like a statement long since recognized as erroneous. [3]

That last repercussive sentence may have to be read twice before it yields its meaning. Transforming an admision of crucial error into an implication of advance, it advises us that a major theory, still a major source of income for psychoanalysts, had by 1929 been long withdrawn. Not withdrawn finally, though, for in 1958 Heinz Hartmann, a former   president   of   the   International   Society   for

Psychoanalysis, advised a symposium at New York University that just such conflicts and their outcomes constituted the "dynamic aspect" of Freudianism.⁴

While Freudians point to such revisions and re-revisions as evidence of Freud's flexibility and honesty, the same revisions warn outsiders of the doctrine's unrivalled plasticity and slipperiness. Question $E = mc^2$, and you have questioned Einstein. Prove the Renaissance a sunny emancipation from medieval darkness, and you have brought down in ruin the reconstruction of the Renaissance begun by Jacob Burckhardt and the reconstruction of the Middle Ages still going on. Freud gave us nothing so fixed and definite to lay hold of. It seems in fact to have been his death alone that gave any of his theories finality. Consensus on so amorphous a teaching can hardly be hoped for. With that *caveat* we proceed.

Freud grew up in a late 19th-century environment whose intellectuals commonly felt that Darwin had shown man to be an animal no different from any other save in the complexity of his brain and neural system. Many also felt that science, given free rein, could in time find out everything worth knowing. Freud absorbed that naturalistic, Progressist inheritance as confidently as Marx had absorbed the very similar inheritance bequeathed to him by the atheists of the 18th-century Enlightenment. Within that ambience, however, psychologists in Freud's youth differed significantly in basic assumptions from the therapists now known as psychiatrists.

Psychologists focussed their attention on mental processes, on thinking. Thanks largely to Darwin again, they had begun to consider the mental traits that men shared with other animals. In the 1890's for example, Havelock Ellis had begun publishing his multi-volume

Studies in the Psychology of Sex. Pierre Janet had given the same subject due attention. Psychologists had also begun to consider the mind's unconscious workings.

No more than Marx had been the first to recognize the impact of economics on history was Freud the first to recognize what is now called "the unconscious." Plato, in fact, had recognized it with his figure of man as a charioteer drawn by one obedient and one unruly horse. In the 17th century Thomas Hobbes had perceived a hidden lust for dominion in Puritan religiosity. Early in the 19th century Schopenhauer had pronounced, not fact and reason, but will, appetite, and temperament the determinants of conscious thought. In the 1870's Nietzsche had attributed ascetic ideals to an unconscious will-to-power. In Freud's own time William James described the history of philosophy as the story of a "clash of human temperaments."

Concerned to cure mental disorders, psychiatrists had taken quite a different tack. Psychiatrists were committed to the principle that mental disorders would prove reducible to strictly physiological dysfunctions of the brain. But only with brain syphilis, successfully treated with malarial infusions, had psychiatric therapy been founded on a solid knowledge of causes: the spirochetes causing brain syphilis had been identified, and malaria killed them. Elsewhere, successful therapy had been woefully rare.

As a practicing neurologist Freud sided originally with the physiological presumption, but in the 1880's the unexpected relief of the case of hysteria reported in his and Joseph Breuer's *Studies in Hysteria* of 1895 converted him to the psychologists' way of thinking. Breuer had persuaded a patient to recollect and re-experience in a state of hypnosis the circumstances of her symptoms' origin and the emotions accompanying it. In apparent response to that proceeding the symptoms disappeared. From this Freud concluded that neurotic symptoms were psychologically induced. Whence his initial claim to have freed psychiatry from physiology.[5]

Once committed to the study of mental processes, Freud attracted attention by his writings. In these he stated that "mental processes are essentially unconscious, and . . . those which are conscious are merely isolated acts and parts of the whole."[6] At the same time he sexualized the unconscious and declared it the long looked-for source of mental disorders. These propositions emerged in *The Interpretation of Dreams* in 1900 and, over the next few years, in *Three Essays on Sexuality* and other publications. Concurrently, he and his admirers claimed that the same propositions were confirmed by his and his pupils' success in actual treatment of patients. By 1910 that alleged success, possibly aided by the gaminess of his theories and their affront to traditional mores, had made psychoanalysis the basis of an enthusiastic international movement. Thereafter, Freud devoted a long life to revising his doctrine, elaborating it, denouncing those heretics who rejected or deviated from it, and furthering the movement it inspired. Though making only modest headway in Europe, the doctrine Freud had developed by the time of World War I prospered mightily in an America eager for progress in every field.

Central to that doctrine and the ground of its therapeutic promise was a sharply compartmentalized conception of the human mind and a predominantly or wholly sexual conception of human maturation.

Freud derived all thought and action from instincts of bodily origin seated in the unconscious, which last he described as by far the mind's greater part and one shut off from consciousness. The instincts seated in it normally made their way into consciousness as impulses prompting conscious action.[7] Such impulse first revealed itself in the feral, lawless craving for pleasure that in the individual appears at birth. Freud gave that familiar craving the name of "libido," declared it sexual at bottom, and pronounced it the lifelong driving force of man. He declared it complemented only by a prudential "ego" that steered the libido-driven individual clear of dangers in the external world.[8]

So motivated and guided in Freud's belief, the maturing human passed through a sequence of phases in which the libido found satisfaction in different objects. In the early phases of growth these objects were areas of the individual's own body. The first of these was the mouth, where infants discovered that in addition to obtaining nourishment by sucking the mother's breast they could obtain pleasure in the simple act of sucking, as in sucking their thumbs. The next bodily area selected for such "narcissistic" pleasure was the anus, where, Freud emphasized, infants obtained pleasure in defecating and in dabbling in their feces and soiling themselves. At that point children were called upon to conform to parental standards, and here in Freud's belief much later personality was formed. For example, too easy and forgiving a toilet training would produce untidiness and prodigality in later life, while too strict a training would produce excessive neatness and frugality—although, Freud warned, "reaction formations" might occur and produce a complete reversal of those results. Here, as very often in Freudian psychology, the same cause might produce contrary results.

In the early years of childhood onanistic pleasure in the sex organs also appeared, as did various mild perversions that normally faded away—but might unfold into perverted sexuality later. At this stage, too, a boy's libido began to center on his mother, and though he normally identified with his father he also began to resent his father's claims on his mother's attention. A girl's libido moved her in opposite but corresponding directions.

Meanwhile the ego formed. Taking increasing account of the external world, the ego normally effected a child's transition from uncontrolled infantile pursuit of pleasure to a pursuit of pleasure guided by the "reality principle."

At puberty, when the sexual instinct came on in full strength, the libido normally found its object in members of the opposite sex. At this time a boy's earlier attachment to his mother, and a girl's to her father, unfolded in an overtly sexual "Oedipus complex." A boy now craved sexually to possess his mother and, Freud did not hesitate to say, to murder his father, while a girl nursed corresponding cravings. Normally, however, the boy feared castration by his father and so gave up his designs on his mother and sought a libidinal object outside the family. Fearing loss of her mother's love, the girl made a similar adjustment. For both, as Freud saw it, the great task of maturation was to free themselves from the Oedipus complex. Once this was done, once libidinal desire had found a non-incestuous object, boy and girl had successfully taken the step to "genital character" and thus, in the Freudian view, attained what had traditionally required earning a living or making a home, adult manhood and womanhood. Thereafter, one gathers, they would pursue and find their prime satisfaction in genital arousal and discharge.

Freud emphasized that in each phase of the above maturation process obstacles and frustrations had to be overcome. The growing human had first to make his peace with toilet training, then to adjust to external reality, and finally to give up a parent (sometimes a sibling) as libidinal object and find an object in the outside world. Neuroses typically arose when the individual failed to solve the problems posed and obtain libidinal pleasure in prudent or parentally approved ways. On such occasions, instead of confronting and redirecting desires that violated parental norms or threatened personal safety, the failing individual made a "vehement effort" to deny the troubling desire's entrance into consciousness.[9] Thus repressed, they returned to their source in the unconscious, "a special region of the mind, shut off from the rest." Dammed up there and unreachable by ordinary memory, but charged with energy, they afflicted the individual, perhaps years later, with the irrational dislikes and fears, tics and odd compulsions, characteristic of neuroses. Yet they also, Freud maintained, appeared in disguised and, like the results of toilet training, in sometimes contrary forms in dreams and random association of ideas. There, psychoanalysts privy to their disguises and contrarieties could identify them and trace their repression to events in the individual's personal history.

Therapy consisted in presenting such identification to the patient via interpretation of his dreams and association of ideas until, overcoming resistance to the interpretations mounted by the fear or repulsion that had effected the repression in the first place, the patient acknowledged that the analyst had correctly identified the repressed material. By thus confessing repellent or dangerous desires the patient brought them into consciousness and thereby disarmed them. Thereafter he or she could seek libidinal satisfaction in a fashion safer or more respectable. Artistic and scientific achievement, for example, had its source in and represented sublimations of an infant's wanton desire to dabble in its feces.

What this teaching meant to many members of the psychoanalytical movement comes clear in this encomium:

> If Darwin anchored man in [primordial] slime, it was Freud who brought a truth even more difficult to accept: beneath the outer crust of man's civilized personality Freud pried open the volcanic cauldron of violent, possessive, unreasoning, and primitive impulses which he insisted are man's real nature. But if Freud stripped man of his illusions and dignity, he offered a way of winning them back. Through self-knowledge, courage, growth, the barbarian could be pacified . . . the civilized fortified.[10]

Let us waive the slip in writing "them" in the penultimate sentence above, which makes illusions as well as dignity the Freudian legacy. The encomiast then advises us that the courage we display in embracing Freud's account of our real nature, plus the self-knowledge and maturity achieved on the couch, will uplift and civilize the essential "barbarian" in us. In Freud's insistence on the ultimacy of biological impulse the usually sober literary critic Lionel Trilling discovered an even greater value. Anxious that civilization itself not be made an absolute, yet unable to find a counterpoise in religion, Trilling acclaimed Freud for enabling men to find the needed counterpoise in submission to biological impulse. In bedroom and presumably bathroom Freud's beneficiaries would find the freedom from human authority and circumstance once found at the altar rail.

Whatever one thinks of that, it is evident that Freud envisioned constant conflict between the individual's libido and ego, and though in Freud's opinion that conflict did not necessarily issue in crippling neurosis, it often did in his and his followers' opinion issue in the irrationalities and warped personalities that "progressive" moderns suspect in "reactionaries." A world abreast of psychoanalysis would rid itself of such impedimenta. Thus Freud raised hope of human minds as clear-cut, practical, and frictionless as well designed machines and therefore fit at last to bid good-bye to the evils of the past.

*   *   *

In reading the above account of Freud's doctrine the reader may have found it hard to believe that instinctual drives of bodily origin sufficiently account for the arts and industries, creeds and sciences, wars and genocides of our restless and inventive species. Did Freud ignore most of what is most significant and interesting about the human race? In any event it is evident that so instinctivist a view of human nature rebounds as fatally against its own claim to rationality and truth as do the instinctivisms advanced by Marx and Darwin. If, whether consciously or not, men strive constantly and only to satisfy their instincts, what can their thought and action be but efforts, however masked and indirect, toward that commanding end? Will they not accept as truth whatever serves attainment of that end? Freud acknowledged the existence of a deeply rooted human belief in psychic freedom and choice, but he termed it "quite unscientific" and declared that it "must give way before the claims of a determinism which governs even mental life."''

"No matter!" we may be told by people chiefly interested in Freudianism's original claim to attention. "As therapy, does psychoanalysis work?"

There is no doubt that the psychoanalytical movement owed much of its early dynamism to psychoanalysis's alleged effectiveness in the treatment of mental disorders. In fact, however, that effectiveness has never been convincingly confirmed. It fairly can be said that psychoanalysis's alleged therapeutic successes have been uncritically assumed or, in the aggregate, carried by appeal to World Opinion.

Freud's own writings detail the treatment of only five patients. Two of these five failed even in his own estimation to improve, and he made little effort to ascertain whether the improvement claimed for the others resulted from his treatment or from some external cause. He unswervingly refused to make full disclosure of his clinical results. The Psychoanalytical Association itself has remarked the same reluctance on the part of psychoanalysts generally.[12] But to determine psychoanalysis's therapeutic value we need not rely on the implications of such reluctance. Once well established as the sage of an international movement, Freud dropped broader and broader hints that the therapeutic value of psychoanalysis had been exaggerated—by whom he did not say. In 1932 he stated, "I do not believe our successes can compare with those of Lourdes,"[13] which last, as a lifelong atheist, he was hardly prone to magnify.

The wisdom of that withdrawal of his initial claims has been shown by every careful effort to investigate the question. In the 1930's, an entire generation after Freud had first made his claims, it was not Freud or a Freudian but P. G. Denker, M.D., of New York who at last launched that surely obligatory investigation. Dr. Denker followed the histories of several hundred neurotic people who had been treated only by general medical practitioners. He made the comforting discovery that within a period of two years roughly two-thirds of these people had recovered.[14] Another investigation took place a few years later in California, where one group of neurotic people was treated by psychoanalysis while a second, matched group received no treatment at all. Both groups improved to nearly the same degree.

In 1975 R. Bruce Sloane, Chairman of the Department of Psychiatry at the University of Southern California medical school, organized what is probably the most recent and carefully conducted investigation of psychoanalysis's therapeutic effectiveness. Concerned to compare the results of behavioral therapy, which relies on conditioning and ignores the unconscious, with the results of psychoanalysis, Dr. Sloane and his co-workers interviewed several dozen psychiatric out-patients and assigned them to three matched groups. One group received behavioral treatment, another received psychoanalytical treatment, and the third group was put on a "waiting list." After several months all were interviewed again and examined for results. Those treated behaviorally seemed slightly better off than the others, but no significant difference appeared between those treated psychoanalytically and those still on the "waiting list."[15]

While such investigations face difficulty in determining what constitutes improvement or cure, they deserve attention for respecting what countless psychoanalysts claiming therapeutic success have not respected, the elementary principle of controlled clinical test. That a person or a group improves with a given therapy means nothing unless a similar person or group fails to improve without it. Yet critical minds require more: to establish a treatment's effectiveness, improvement when it does occur must be shown to follow from the treatment and not from some other cause or, as Dr. Denker's results suggest, from the passage of time. In fact, improvement sometimes occurs not only with countless different varieties of psychoanalysis but also with well over two hundred different kinds of non-psychoanlytical psychotherapies.[16]

Gestalt therapists, Bio-Energetic therapists, Reality therapists, Sex therapists, Primal Scream therapists, and others gaudier still claim successes that are as well confirmed as those claimed by psychoanalysts. Moreover, people allegedly helped or cured by these other therapies come to believe quite as firmly in the explanations given them for their improvement as do those allegedly helped by psychoanalysis. The amount of spurious self-knowledge now at large in America may well exceed our knowledge of the arts and sciences. All comes very close to proving that any therapy whatever, solemnly administered, can sometimes serve effectively as a placebo. Demanding investment of more time and money than the others, and wrapped in an imposing language, psychoanalysis may in theory have an edge for those who can afford it. Every general practitioner knows the principle.

The general practitioner also knows that in cases of emotional distress a hired friend may be better than no friend at all. He may not cure, but he may give the healing power of time or of native common sense an opportunity. Dr. Sloane suggests that the human relationship with the therapist *is* the therapy. But cure was the initial claim. It has never been substantiated.

The evidence pretty clearly indicates that most neurotics recover with the passage of time and that psychoanalysis has no more effect on their disorders or on the disorders of the unfortunates who do not recover than aspirin or a purge. In 1964 William B. Sargant, former President of the Psychiatric Section of England's Royal College of Medicine, described England's considerable success in dealing with mental disorders with the help of drugs. Comparing that success with America's notorious failure in treating the same disorders, Sargant accounted for the latter by citing the U.S. government's and the Rockefeller and Ford Foundations' heavyhanded promotion of psychoanalysis in American mental hospitals and university medical centers. Dr. Sargant wrote:

> The same amount of money, or even a tenth of it, spent on the much more practical medical and biochemical approaches to the treatment of the mentally ill would have produced a revolution in conditions in American mental hospitals similar to that which occurred in British mental hospitals.[17]

We have, however, only begun to plumb the bent and substance of a uniquely fluid doctrine.

Before withdrawing his therapeutic claims Freud had in the 1920's, as we earlier saw Professor Hall remarking, revamped his theory of motivation. This he did in 1920 with publication of *Beyond the Pleasure Principle*. That volume announced discovery of an instinct for self-destruction or death instinct, which then took its place in Freudianism beside the pleasure-seeking libido as a fundamental human motor.[18]

Originally, Freud had pointed to psychoanalysis's alleged therapeutic success as proof of the correctness of his theory of unconscious libidinal motivation. Only, he had reasoned, if psychoanalysis's explanations of neuroses were correct, would cures result. This was not quite true, because, as we have seen, cures might also result from the passage of time. On the other hand, it was true that if psychoanalytical theory were correct, cures *would* result. And by 1920 Freud had begun to suspect that cures seldom did result. In that situation he seems to have told himself that fault lay not in psychoanalysis but—*verdammt!*—in mankind's basic incurability, its innate self-destructiveness. In any event, the attribution of a death instinct to mankind immediately following World War I performed yeoman service for psychoanalysis and the movement. It transformed therapeutic failure into a new cause for congratulation. Freud claimed an exciting new psychological discovery: man not only craved libidinal pleasure; he also wanted to destroy himself.

That and similar performances moved P. B. Medawar, an uncommonly erudite winner of a Nobel Prize in medicine, to pronounce Freudianism "the most stupendous intellectual confidence trick of the 20th century."[19] The present writer does not go so far. Incredible as it may seem to a mind of Medawar's caliber, the shift of ground described above seems to have soothed and satisfied Freud himself as effectively as it did his admirers. Freud surely was "sincere."

The new breakthrough freed psychoanalysis from the nagging demand for results that any therapy must satisfy. It also vastly enlarged psychoanalysis's scope. It transformed psychoanalysis from a therapy to a comprehensive system of psychology that covered factory and office, battlefield and highway, as well as nursery, bathroom, and bedroom. In the course of this transformation of his doctrine Freud introduced an "id" as the source and reservoir of unconscious psychic energy, made the libido representative not only of the sex drive but of others not originally recognized, and added to the prudential ego a "super-ego," analogous to Marx's spiritual superstructure, composed of whatever morality and ideals had been implanted by parents, teachers, and society. "The social instincts," Freud wrote, echoing Darwin's reply to Wallace about the moral sense or conscience, "are not regarded as elementary or irreducible."[20] In Freudianism conscience reduced to an interiorization of the conventions of any given time or place.

In an *Encyclopaedia Britannica* article, "Psychoanalysis" of 1929, Freud advised, "The future will probably attribute far more importance to psychoanalysis as the science of the unconscious than as a therapeutic procedure." He went on in the same article to applaud the new science, not for achieving cures, but for making clear "for the first time [*sic*] the difficulties in the way of cures."[21] In the end Freud presented psychoanalysis not as therapy but as pure science.

Now we earlier noted that the myriad theories constituting Freudian psychology seldom offer stable objects for investigation. In addition, or in consequence, a critic of Freudianism is often told that he has aimed his fire at false versions of the doctrine, usually at "pop psychoanalysis." Yet when he asks for authentic Freudianism he is often given something that is true enough and even worth heeding but by no means distinctively or uniquely Freudian, for example the truth that we sometimes overlook our real motives. In hope of avoiding such a dead end we shall fasten on the three theories on which, according to Freud's pupil and biographer Ernest Jones, Freud himself put greatest store. These three are his libido theory, the Oedipus complex, and the interpretation of dreams. We consider them in that order, and will then consider Freud's cardinal notion of repression.

In originally conceiving the libido as sexual, Freud's libido theory found the springs of human thought and action solely in man's animal nature. So doing, the theory really did little more than assert that man was an instinct-driven animal like any other, little more than deny that man had been created in the image of a free God. The theory did little more than express the atheism that Freud directly vented in 1930 in his book on religion, *The Future of an Illusion*.

As time went on, however, Freud was forced to admit the existence of drives with little sexual content. In consequence he revised his conception of the libido and made it represent not only sexual desire but also "self-love . . . love for parents and children, friendship, and love for humanity in general, and also devotion to concrete objects and abstract ideas."[22] Examining that omnicompetent conception a generation ago, J. W. N. Sullivan, a man trained in physics, observed:

> Such a concept as Freud's libido . . . is called upon to explain so much that it explains nothing. So far as scientific explanation is concerned, no more is gained by saying that the most diverse manifesttions all come about through the libido than by saying that they all come about through the will of God.[23]

The outstanding sociologist P. A. Sorokin remarked much the same:

> Freud's [libido] conception and theory give us no more than the statement: "The life-activities of man and society are the function and manifestation of the life factor . . . ."[24]

The addition of an instinct for death and destruction in the 1920's gave us only the statement that an instinct for destruction accounted for man's destructive activities. Untenable in its original formulation, the libido theory proves empty in its later formulation.

As laid down by Freud, the Oedipus theory did make a substantial statement: at puberty every son longed to murder his father and replace him in the marriage bed (though a sister's bed might sometimes serve), and every daughter harbored corresponding longings. "The most stringent prohibitions," Freud warned, "are required to prevent this . . . tendency from being carried into effect."[25]

There, if true, was substantial knowledge definitely new. In fact, one doubts that any sober mind ever accepted it. Many a boy has considered rapping the paternal skull with some blunt instrument, but not to the point of murder, and almost none have found their toil-worn mothers as appetizing as the high-school cheerleader. By now most psychoanalysts have perceived the theory's palpable untruth. Erich Fromm for example has written that the Oedipus theory must be reinterpreted to signify no more than the desire of growing boys and girls to escape parental authority. Fromm, who is also an interpretive editor of Marx, neglects to say why we should reinterpret the theory into a platitude insted of simply forgetting it. "Nature is pleased with simplicity," wrote Isaac Newton, "and affects not the pomp of superfluous causes."

Of Freud's three favorite theories, dream interpretation remains.

During World War II at the University of Minnesota a group of conscientious objectors submitted voluntarily to experiments in starvation in which they lost a quarter of their bodily weight. These men recorded the thoughts of their waking hours, which were obsessively of food. They also recorded their dreams, and these were compared with the dreams of a control group not subjected to starvation. The results harshly contradicted Freud's notion that dreams were wish fulfillments, on which he had based his dream interpretations and his general view of the unconscious: the starved subjects dreamed of food no more than the members of the control group, who ate their fill.[26]

Within the last decade experimental psychologists have dealt another body blow to Freud's facile guess that dreams represented upwellings of forbidden desires. Students of sleep have discovered that infants, who forbid themselves nothing, dream more than anyone else.[27]

Karl Jaspers, a psychiatrist turned philosopher, inaugurated a widely accepted European critique of Freud's asser-

tion of the meaningfulness of every human manifestation, including dreams. Jaspers and others rightly insisted that
much in human life was fortuitous and not expressive of personality. They also pointed out that in Freud's universally
meaningful world it was impossible to dream about such
commonplace objects as cigars or houses, because in Freud's
world dreams about those objects always stood for something
else. (The meanings Freud gave them call to mind the
Hungarian who on being shown Rohrschach inkblots said
they all reminded him of sex. Why? "Because everything
reminds me of sex.") Meanwhile it should be common
knowledge that the same dream submitted to five or ten ac-
credited psychoanalysts will commonly be given five or ten
different meanings.

In 1953 C.P. Oberndorf, in his authoritative *A History
of Psychoanalysis in America*, gently remarked what is still the
case, that "the function and interpretation of the dream remains somewhat of an enigma."

In aggrieved reply to empirical falsifications of Freudian theories psychoanlysts may cite Seymour Fisher and
Roger P. Greenberg's recent *The Scientific Credibility of
Freud's Theories and Concepts*. While perhaps unique among
writers sympathetic to Freud in forthrightly remarking empirical falsifications of many Freudian notions, Fisher and
Greenberg have cheered the psychoanalytical community
by remarking a remainder that facts agree with. They seem
not, however, to understand that more is required of an ac-
ceptable theory than agreement with facts. Thomas
Aquinas, for one, showed awareness of this in suspending
judgement on medieval cosmological theories, which often
agreed well with observed planetary movements. Aquinas
correctly stated that complete agreement with facts could
not prove a theory true, because the same facts might also

agree with some other theory "which men have not yet at all conceived." Mindful of this, sound thinkers desiring to establish a theory, try to demonstrate that it is the only theory from which the facts can be deduced. Freud and his followers made no effort in that direction.

We also may be told that psychoanalysis or "depth psychology" is a new science and that to deny it unlimited forbearance betrays a spirit hostile to scientific inquiry. In truth, psychoanalysis is no longer new. By now much more time has passed since the publication of *The Interpretation of Dreams* in 1900 than passed from Galileo's *Two New Sciences* of 1638 to Newton's *Principia* of 1687.

Given the undermining of its own claim to rationality and truth by any theory that makes bodily satisfaction man's chief or only motive, given also the emptiness of the later libido theory, also the Oedipus complex's dwindling to platitude, and the failure of dream interpretation, one wonders how much that is both new and true can be found in Freudian psychology.

That we are sometimes moved by motives of which we are unaware, and that sexual instinct, when denied satisfaction, can most damnably writhe and rage, few thinking adults have ever doubted. But that childhood desires can remain unaltered in face of later development and experience seems more than doubtful. And that powerful impulses can be repressed into a region of the mind where they become, not simply forgotten, but unreachable by ordinary memory, seems most unlikely. For one thing, sexual desire in particular is supremely conscious, and if, as Freud stated and as seems certain, a vehement effort is required to effect repression, could that effort be unconscious and could it thereafter remain beyond the reach of memory? As evidence for Freud's and other psychoanalysts' key conceptions of an unconscious mind and unconscious repression, we have little more than anecdotal testimony about non-repeatable, not publicly observed, clinical experience; most of this testimony relies on statements elicited from troubled patients by analysts who are partisans of the theory. How really free, one wonders, are the patients' association of ideas? On such dubious evidence hangs the whole Freudian doctrine of repression into an unconscious mind unreachable except by psychoanalysis.

However unconvincing the claims of behaviorism may be, behaviorists like H. J. Eysenk and B. F. Skinner seem well advised in rejecting Freud's science of the unconscious. So do growing numbers of non-Freudian psychiatrists who treat nervous disorders with time, sympathy, and drugs.

In addition to the objections to Freudian psychology noted, others equally well founded have gone blandly ignored by nearly all psychoanalysts. R. R. Sears' scholarly survey in 1942 of Freudian propositions, which Professor Sears summed up as "bad science," still stands unanswered, though occasionally damned, by members of what surely seems a mass movement and not a science.[28] In 1958, early in a university symposium, Ernest Nagel of New York University summarized the huge accumulation of objections that over generations had gone unanswered. Among them was—and is—the one that, while tenable theories generate definite consequences and rule out others, Freudian theories rule out nothing and so accommodate anything that happens. As we saw with regard to toilet training and mentioned in discussion of dream interpretation, the same Freudian cause is claimed to produce and explain contrary effects. What we want, and often obtain from science, are statements in the form of "If A, then B." What we commonly get from Freudianism is "If A, then B or not-B."

Nagel also scored the naiveté of taking as clinical confirmations of dream and other interpretations their acceptance by patients ready to grasp at any straws that promise relief.[29] None of the dozen or so psychoanalysts who later addressed the gathering came to grips with Nagel. The philospher of science Adolf Grünbaum who is also a research professor of psychiatry, has presented similar objections recently.[30]

Well-founded logical and empirical objections receive no serious answer and may never loosen Freudianism's mind-numbing grip on its adherents. The key fact is that, to countless educators and other intellectuals, any definite statement Freud ever made is peripheral and subordinate to his underlying "approach" or "insight." That approach or insight, which we shall consider in our Conclusion, counts; no specific statement matters; and any effort at logical or empirical test stands damned beforehand as based upon a ''crude'' reading of ''the most insightful contribution to our understanding of human nature in the history of humanity.''

But stay! A kind of logic obtains in this indifference to specifics. For if in Freud's collected works authentic scripture cannot be found to show that Freud somewhere revised or re-interpreted or withdrew any theory under consideration, Freudian scripture can be found to show that he transcended it. Freud accomplished this—such is the logic—by withdrawing commitment from all his theories generally. Expressing himself more and more tentatively with the years, he made the various revisions noted at the start of this discussion. In *Beyond the Pleasure Principle* he not only unveiled the death instinct but also admitted crippling exceptions to his principle that dreams were wish fulfillments. In the same volume he wrote that he was not convinced of what he had set forth in it and that he did not ask belief from anyone else.[31] In *The Problem of Anxiety* of 1936, as in his reformulation of the libido theory, he suggested that he had overdrawn his claim of the all-pervasiveness of sexuality.

Supremely difficult to catch, fix, and test on any definite point of doctrine, Freud did exhibit an unwavering commitment about which neither he nor his public seem to have suspected that questions might be asked. This commitment was to his method of instilling agreement and belief. It triply rewards examination because it was also the method used by Darwin and Marx. A passage from Freud's *General Introduction to Psychoanalysis* makes it plain:

> From two selected examples I have now shown you that neurotic symptoms have meaning, like errors and dreams, and that they are clearly related to the events of the patient's life. Can I expect you to believe this exceptionally significant statement on the strength of two examples? No. But can you expect me to go on quoting examples to you until you declare yourselves convinced? Again, no . . . . I will therefore content myself with the examples given and will refer you for more to the literature on the subject . . . .[32]

One can almost hear Freud's rapt audience murmur to itself, "What could be more reasonable than that?" One imagines a similar response when Darwin offers essentially the same argument in his Introduction to *The Origin of Species:*

> I can . . . give only the general conclusions at which I have arrived, with a few facts [examples] in illustration . . . . I shall unfortunately be compelled to treat this subject far too briefly, as it can be treated properly only by giving long catalogues of facts [more examples] . . . .[33]

Although Marx may not have penned an equally revealing statement, his failure to provide a general statement of his doctrine and thus to challenge critical tests left him with examples as his only means of instilling belief.

Thus *The Poverty of Philosophy* exemplifies historical materialism by attributing feudalism to use of the hand-mill, capitalism to use of the steam-mill—while a testing mind remembers that the hand-mill marked pre-industrial societies of every type, while the steam-mill operates today in Soviet Russia. With the *Communist Manifesto*'s narrative of Europe's transition from feudalism to capitalism Marx offered not a test but a lengthy example of historical materialism.

It is a truth accepted by every able thinker that ten thousand examples or pages-long catalogues of supporting facts do not, and cannot, establish a theory, whereas one contradicting instance does upset it. As Darwin correctly wrote, a few examples only illustrate a theory, making clear what it asserts. As Darwin failed to recognize, just the same holds true of any number of examples whatever. Wholly justified as illustrations, examples are and must be selected in the light of the very theory they illustrate. To rely on them to instill belief is not the method of rational thought; it is the method of rhetoric and propaganda. That our Doctors' reliance on it did in fact instill belief in an allegedly educated public constitutes no small criticism of the education that public had received.

Upon reflection everyone will grant that scores of alleged examples can and have been cited in support of all the theories in every field that have been proved false. No one would advance any theory if a great deal did not seem to accord with it. But an able thinker seeks to establish a theory quite the other way round, by *showing that nothing contradicts it*. The principle is basic. It accounts for the relentless tests to which scientists, as opposed to propagandists, subject their own and their colleagues' theories.

What can criticism make of a claimant to scientific distinction, or genius, who presents an all-embracing, morally unsettling, system of psychology, ignores the obligation to test that system, instills belief in it by rhetorical device, and who then busies himself with organizing and promoting a para-religious movement around the same system?[34] What can criticism say of the leader of such a movement who accuses critics of an *"odium sexicum,"* uses his system to pontificate on art and religion, declares it ''the only adequate preparation for the profession of educator,'' demands and gets the faith of troops of innocents, some of them really suffering—and then makes a statement as invertebrate as this one from his *Autobiographical Study* of 1935: ''I can say that I have made many beginnings and thrown out many suggestions. Something will come of them in the future. But I cannot myself tell whether it will be much or little.''[35]

By now, surely, we can tell what has come of Freud's ''beginnings'' and ''suggestions,'' which years earlier had been announced as conclusive psychological discoveries.

It can be said that Freudianism sometimes usefully directed attention to the undoubted fact that men are sometimes moved by motives other than the ones they acknowledge. But after La Rochefoucauld, Hobbes, Schopenhauer, Nietzsche, Marx, and many other probers of human nature, that service cannot be called at all unique.

A stronger case than any for Freudianism can be made for Freud himself and grounded in his abandonment of the Progressism that he had uncritically absorbed from the intellectual climate of his youth. Toward the end of his life, no longer expecting psychoanalysis to rid the world of unreason, he wrote that ''we shall still have to struggle for

an incalculable time with the difficulties which the un-
tameable character of human nature presents . . . . ''[36]
Unlike Darwin and especially Marx, Freud came to
acknowledge that human nature was not about to change,
that man was born to trouble as sparks fly upward. Unfortunately, but typically, even as in 1935 he voiced that cau-
tionary good sense, Freud opined that ''the revolution in
Russia — in spite of all its disagreeable details — seems like a
message of a better future.''[37] Unfortunately too, it was
much less the aged and sometimes sober Freud than the early dreamreader and sexological fisher in the unconscious
who left his mark on 20th-century thought and conduct.

Largely on the basis of *Civilization and Its Discontents*,
which Freud published in 1930, Freud has sometimes been
viewed as an advocate of the instinctual renunciation which
that book declares a necessity of civilization. Thus some
have acclaimed Freud as a great civilizational hero. Decades
earlier, however, he had launched his movement by giving
the instinctive, animal element in human nature unprecedented weight. He had given sexual satisfaction in particular a value never given it before and had warned that
failure to achieve such satisfaction led to some or severe
neurosis. Historically, aside from riveting many minds to
sterile focus on self and personal feelings, the most obvious
result of psychoanalysis has been a ''new morality'' subversive of civilization generally.

Beyond that, Freudianism, here apeing Marxism, has
seemed to legitimize that most vicious of rhetorical devices,
argument *ad hominem*. Confronted with ideas unwelcome to
them in any field from art to politics, Freud's legatees find it
all too easy to ask, not if such ideas might be true, but why,
in terms of personality, their spokesmen adhere to them

—and to answer that question with personal derogation. Deliberative thought comes to be taken not as an attempt to describe or understand the world but as involuntary expression of personal history and temperament, perhaps of toilet training. Thus Freudianism poisons the springs of rational discussion, shelters fondly held opinions from reality, and leaves force the likely means of settling disputes. All this despite the obvious fact that people of the most diverse personal histories and temperaments often hold the same ideas, while people of similar personal histories and temperaments often differ, and while still other people change their ideas without changing their personal histories or temperaments. Freudian psychologism to the contrary, human thought can no more be accounted for as mere expression of personal history than it can be accounted for as mere expression of class membership.

In the realm of psychological theory, Freud's "suggestions" have inspired a truly appalling proliferation of untested, mutually conflicting hypotheses, each of them occasioned by the failure of the others. Starting with the Jungian and Adlerian, and continuing with the Rankian, Reichian, and other revolts, all of them met by venomous *ad hominem* attack, Freudian psychology has become a churning, chain-reacting cloud of facile guesses out of which conflicting guesses still burst and billow in all directions. At the cloud's center the original cluster of guesses, Freud's own, has since his death been so revised, re-revised, contradicted, and, to mix a metaphor for what is unbelievably mixed in fact, so variously parboiled, marinated, fricasseed, and hashed that it no longer possesses an identity.[38] Nothing beyond platitude has been confirmed; almost nothing has been defined; very little has been tested and that seldom on psychoanalysts' initiative; words like "regression," "transference," "repression," and "psychoanalysis" itself have come to mean whatever any individual psychoanalyst wants them to mean; and opposing lawyers confidently hire psychoanalysts to testify to whatever lawyers want testimony for.[39]

Taken in the round, the psychoanalytical enterprise seems the most subversive of intelligence since the friar Wetzel peddled papal indulgences through 16th-century Wittenberg, thereby lighting Martin Luther's explosive fuse. Psychoanalysis's ultimate defense has long consisted in the assertion, first voiced by Freud, that only those who have been psychoanalyzed, which is to say only true believers, are fit to judge. Said Samuel Johnson, "Madam, nonsense can be defended only by nonsense."

Notes on Chapter III

1. Cited in Percival Bailey, M.D., "The Great Psychiatric Revolution," *American Journal of Psychiatry*, 1956, p. 395.

2. Loc. cit., p. 17.

3. Civilization and Its Discontents, transl. Joan Riviere, The International Psychoanalytical Library, Ernest Jones ed., London, 1949, pp. 95–96.

4. Hartmann, "Psychoanalysis as a Scientific Theory," in *Psychoanalysis, Scientific Method, and Philosophy*, Sidney Hook ed., 1959, p. 10.

5. Cf. Freud's Introduction to his *Introductory Lectures on Psychoanalysis* in *The Complete Introductory Lectures on Psychoanalysis*, James Strachey ed., 1966, p. 21. (The latter volume contains both the Introductory Lectures of 1915–17 and the New Introductory Lectures of 1933.)

6. Freud, *A General Introduction to Psychoanalysis* (the first series of lectures), revised ed., transl. Joan Riviere, 1935, p. 22.

7. Ibid., p. 260f. Also Lecture XXI of *Complete Lectures, op. cit.*

8. *Ibid.*, pp. 285–96 present Freud's description of the maturation process.

9. Ibid., p. 259.

10. Leo Cherne's encomium in *The Saturday Review of Literature*, Sept. 27, 1958.

11. Complete Introductory Lectures, op. cit., pp. 106, 49.

12. *Bulletin of The American Psychoanalytical Association*, 1952. C. P. Oberndorf, *A History of Psychoanalysis in America*, 1953, remarks the same.

13. Freud, *The Complete Introductory Lectures, op. cit.*, pp. 397–98.

14. Denker, "Results of Treatment of Psychoneuroses by the General Practitioner," in *New York State Journal of Medicine,* 1946.

15. Sloane *et al. Psychotherapy Versus Behavior Therapy,* 1975. Behaviorists ignore the unconscious and attempt to alter sequences of behavior by conditioning. In England H. J. Eysenck, in America B. F. Skinner, seem the behviorists most referred to.

16. Cf. R. Herink, *The Psychotherapy Handbook: The A to Z Guide to 250 Different Therapies in Use Today,* 1980.

17. Sargant, "Psychiatric Treatment Here and in England," *Atlantic Monthly,* July, 1964.

18. Beyond the Pleasure Principle, vol. XVIII of the Standard Edition of The Complete Psychological Works of Sigmund Freud, transl. and ed. James Strachey, 1955, pp. 34–60.

19. Medawar in *The New York Review of Books,* Jan. 23, 1975, p. 17.

20. Freud's article, "Psychoanalysis," in *The Encyclopaedia Britannica,* 1929 (repeated in later editions).

21. Ibid.

22. Freud, *Group Psychology and the Analysis of the Ego,* in vol. XVIII of the Standard Edition of the Complete Psychological Works of Sigmund Freud, *op. cit.,* p. 90.

23. Sullivan, *The Limitations of Science,* 1933, p. 121; see also p. 127.

24. Pitirim Sorokin, *Contemporary Sociological Theories,* 1928, p. 607.

25. A General Introduction to Psychoanalysis, 1920 edition, transl. Joan Riviere, p. 294.

26. J. Brozek *et al.,* in *Journal of Personality,* 1951, pp. 256–57.

27. See for example Edwin Diamond, author of *The Science of Sleep,* in *New York Times Magazine,* Feb. 12, 1967.

28. Sears, "Survey of Objective Studies of Psychoanalytical Concepts," in Bulletin 51, 1943, of the Social Science Research Council.

29. Nagel's contribution to *Psychoanalysis, Scientific Method, and Philosophy, op. cit.*

30. See Professor Grünbaum's substantial letter in *Commentary,* November, 1980, p. 21.

31. Beyond the Pleasure Principle, op. cit., p. 59.

32. Loc. cit., p. 238. See also p. 262, *passim.*

33. Loc. cit.

34. See Freud's criticism of "conventional sexual morality" in his *General Introduction, op. cit.,* p. 377.

35. Freud, *An Autobiographical Study,* transl. James Strachey, 2nd. ed., London, 1946, p. 130.

36. Complete Introductory Lectures, op. cit., p. 645.

37. Ibid., p. 645.

38. Seymour Fisher and Roger P. Greenberg, *The Scientific Credibility of Freud's Theories and Concepts,* 1977, observes that "the diversity of the secondary elaboration of Freud's ideas is . . . . Babel-like." G.S. Blum, *Psychoanalytical*

Theories of Personality, 1952, collects a wide variety of secondary elaborations and correctly notes that psychoanalysts typically concoct new theories rather than test any.

39. E.g., Whittaker Chambers, *Witness* (Chicago: Henry Regnery, 1952) p. 691n.

Conclusion

Revisions and withdrawals have made it difficult to state what in the end, though by no means in their beginnings, our three Doctors meant to say. At one moment Darwin with his selection theory of evolution, Marx with historical materialism, and Freud with his science of the unconscious deny man's rationality and mental freedom; at another moment they claim in their own persons freely and rationally to lay bare the nature of the human race; at still a third moment their withdrawals leave their statements with very little meaning at all.

One does not suggest that disproof of the central doctrines mentioned disproves everything their authors presented with them. In all three writers some wisdom can be found. Once he had withdrawn his therapeutic claims Freud occasionally took a view of mankind's future sufficiently realistic to earn him the suspicion of visionary socialists. Though unable adequately to explain the rise of capitalism, let alone its consequences, Marx did perceive more clearly than many men today the historicity and hence impermanence of any existing social or economic order. Beyond performing a public service in scuttling the special creation notion that a maleducated public had fallen into, Darwin included in *The Origin of Species* a brief but fine description of the interdependence of living creatures and their environment that may some day replace evolution as biology's unifying principle.[1] But it was our Doctors' central, most distinctive and charismatic doctrines and those doctrines' devaluation of human mind and reason in favor of animal instinct that, along with their paradoxical promise of human progress, got implanted in modernity.

This question now demands an answer: how could doctrines as empirically and logically flawed as the ones that we have considered capture the assent of the best minds of the late 19th and early 20th centuries? The answer to that question is brief and incontestable: the doctrines we have considered did not in fact capture such minds' assent. Marx and Freud never came close to capturing the assent of such men as Max Weber, Werner Sombart, Pierre Janet, William James, Ortega y Gasset, P. A. Sorokin, and Karl Popper. *The Origin of Species* as Darwin finally left it devotes most of its pages to arguing against the objections raised by contemporary scientists. Darwin's most prestigious supporter, the geologist Lyell, repeatedly annoyed Darwin by the lukewarmness of his support. T. H. Huxley ended in profound doubt and attempts to repair his philosophical innocence.

Millions of lesser minds, however, did enthusiastically assent. Part of the explanation surely lies in this: mass education and mass journalism were bringing millions out of sheer illiteracy and equipping them uncritically to ingest anything made plausible by fluent writers. Moreover by paring away men's decent pride in their humanity, by pronouncing them creatures of circumstance and instinct, do you not most pleasurably license them to follow every impulse that safely can be followed, to exploit every opportunity for pleasure or personal advancement? Go on, as some educators have gone on, to tell people that acceptance of that license evidences an insight deeper than the ordinary and characterizes brave champions of human progress—do all that, and you have constructed a temptation equalling Eve's and not much different.

Less obvious, perhaps, but undoubtedly contributing to our Doctors' popular success was their time's religion. Once viewing man and society with the unflinching realism of Hebrew prophets and Christian Fathers, the religion of even the better educated had grown shallow and soft. Against the teaching of the Church's greatest Doctors, religionists were taking Bible language literally, and nature's beauty and alleged benevolence had become common arguments for God. A letter Darwin wrote in 1860 reflects the religion of his time and goes far to explain the welcome then, and still, accorded doctrines hostile to religion:

> I had no intention to write atheistically. But I own that I cannot see as plainly as others do, and as I should wish to do, evidence of design and beneficence on all sides of us. There seems to me too much misery in the world. I cannot persuade myself that a benevolent and omnipotent God would have designedly created the *Ichneumonidae* with the express intention of their feeding within the living bodies of caterpillars, or that a cat should play with mice.[2]

Extended to human affairs, such considerations ruined the argument from design that had become a religious staple. In his *Natural Theology* of 1802, which had gone through edition after edition, that argument had moved the Anglican theologian William Paley to express himself this way:

> It is a happy world after all. The air, the earth, the water teem with delighted existence . . . . [Insects, fish, other

creatures] are so happy that they know not what to do with themselves.[3]

Considerations like Darwin's destroyed the argument, as does consideration of the often frightful course of human history. Meanwhile even the better educated seem not to have known that no canonical writer had relied on such an argument, that the faith of Hebrew prophets and Christian Fathers had quite other springs. Few seem to have remembered that Jewish belief in God flourished in a nation repeatedly victimized by its larger neighbors and that Christianity arose in a society that had crucified the Christian Savior and for centuries martyred his followers. The authentic Judeo-Christian argument has not been from nature or the world to God but from inner experience—of freedom and conscience—to God, *despite* nature and the world.

It was with a public sufficiently educated to reject a religion fit at best for children, yet a public philosophically naive and theologically illiterate, that Darwinism, Marxism, and Freudianism scored their historical success. And in all three instances the same sequence of events occurred: first, sensational announcements destructive of traditional thought and feeling; then insuperable objections forcing large, even comprehensive, withdrawals; and finally endless revision, equivoation, and the stubborn assertion that if, in any literal ("crude") reading, the announcements stand disproved, still there is enormous value in them. This last constitutes the soft or sophisticated position mentioned in this book's Introduction.

In very nearly its entirety the biological profession consists today of men and women aware of, if not Darwinism's logical rebound against its own claim to rationality, at least most of its other failings. Today biologists recognize natural selection as a secondary pruning, not a primary creating, process. They acknowledge the inability of sexual selection to account for the persistence of non-useful characteristics. They know that neither competitive selection nor social institutions can change the human genotype; they know that only gene mutation can change it and that for ages it has not changed. They also acknowledge what strikes hard at the modern or synthetic theory of evolution, the lack of survival value in many new organs' initial stages. One supposes them aware of the species barrier, of the mathematical odds against evolution by natural selection of random mutations, and of the fundamental discontinuities remarked by Goldschmidt and du Noüy. Yet while doubting or disclaiming most of Darwinism and everything distinctive of it, many of them pay and call on us to pay homage to Darwin as the equal of Newton or Einstein. Thus Stephen Jay Gould of Harvard rejects Darwinian gradualism, correctly writes that "the essence of Darwinism lies in its claim that natural selection creates the fit," styles himself "not one of the most ardent defenders of natural selection"—and yet makes himself one of the most ardent defenders of Darwin.[4]

Exemplifying soft Marxism, R.K. Merton of Columbia readily admits the validity of most of the objections to Marxism as a sociology or theory of history, but at the same time Merton accepts Marxism as a "general orientation." The difference between accepting Marxism as a sociology and accepting it as a general orientation seems more than tenuous, especially when we find Merton faulting Sorokin's sociology for failing to incorporate Marx's notion that class determines thinking.[5]

Walter Kaufmann of Princeton rightly castigated Freud's notion of science as a sublimation of infants' alleged desire to dabble in their feces. (Infants dabble in anything.)

But Kaufmann went on to pronounce Freud, for reasons not stated, "a great enlightener."[6]

Clearly, something other than devotion to tested knowledge inspires the soft warrantors of our Doctors' extraordinary genius.

Basically at issue, functioning as a fundamental principle and accounting for the persistent adulation of writers whose crucial errors and inadequacies are increasingly admitted, is philosophical naturalism and what that comes down to, atheism. Though almost no one says this, will not reflective people quickly perceive its truth? Is it not in academia at least an open secret?

Though by no means the first modern writers to conceive man and all his works immured within and components of the closed, self-sufficient universe of natural causes envisioned, or thought to be envisioned, by the science of their day, in varying that theme as they respectively varied it Darwin, Marx, and Freud created enormous public stir. Implanting in newly literate millions a proud rejection of what, unbeknownst to the same millions, Jewish rabbis and Christian Doctors also had rejected, Darwin, Marx, and Freud became the standard-bearers of a great, popular, half-educated campaign of naturalistic enlightenment.

Declaring the nature investigated by modern science the whole of reality, denying any transcendence of that nature, naturalism attributes human life in all its aspects to the ordinary operation of that same nature. In such a view human beings can only think and act, not rationally or freely, but as natural causes compel them to. Here, in naturalism, is the root of the logical rebound against their own claims to rationality and truth in which we have found Darwinism, Marxism, and Freudianism hopelessly entangled. Here also lies immense danger: naturalism invites us to

treat our fellow men like cattle. Yet here, also, is the enormous value that we are asked to find and treasure in our
three Doctors. To promote naturalism, which comes down
to atheism, seems the frequent intent and surely is the effect
of the soft Darwinism, soft Marxism, and soft Freudianism
urged on college youth and the reading public.

Pressed to justify what is clearly a philosophic rather
than a scientific commitment, soft Darwinians, Marxists,
and Freudians commonly offer one reply. It is that by opening up biology, sociology, and psychology to naturalistic inquiry Darwin, Marx, and Freud freed those studies from
religiously inspired paralysis and thereby cleared the way for
later scientific advance.

In truth, as mention of such early evolutionists as
Lamarck, Diderot, and Erasmus Darwin, and of such social
scientists as Saint-Simon, Ricardo, and Fourier, and of
psychologists such as Wundt, MacDougall, or James should
suffice to show, the studies in question had not been
paralyzed. The men named and many others had asked fer-
tile questions and advanced some still tenable ideas. The
point to settle is this: did our Doctors' theories make significant contribution to later and truer theories?

We have seen that Darwin contributed neither the idea
of evolution nor the idea of natural selection. His
predecessors had clearly stated both. He contributed, instead, the untenable idea that natural selection *caused* evolution. It was Mendel, not Darwin, who put biologists on
the track to the knowledge of genetics on which the present synthetic theory of evolution rests. And as we have seen
Goldschmidt, du Noüy, molecular biologists, and paleontologists testifying, the synthetic theory itself, largely
because of its Darwinian gradualism, confronts what seem
insurmountable difficulties.

Likewise Marx. As Marx himself acknowledged, earlier writers had remarked the impact of economic affairs on social structure and social conflict. With regard to later writers, Marx contributed nothing to Spengler's and Toynbee's admittedly flawed but sometimes brilliantly suggestive theories of history. Marx contributed no more to what is surely the most conceptually refined and empirically well grounded theory of history extant, the one formulated in Sorokin's *Social and Cultural Dynamics*.

Freud mainly delayed use of the pharmacology that present-day psychiatrists increasingly rely on.

It therefore seems correct to call the vast respect paid Darwin, Marx, and Freud a means of protecting and promoting, despite overwhelming objections to their doctrines, those doctrines' naturalism, or atheism. When biological, sociological, and psychological criticism has winnowed the chaff from those doctrines, little more than previously accepted ideas and naturalism remain. The legacy bequeathed us by our Doctors is philosophic. It consists in the projection of philosophical naturalism, in plain words atheism, into biology, sociology, and psychology.

*   *   *

In recent centuries naturalism has owed much of its appeal to what seems its sanction by modern science. Science, the argument runs, by its very nature seeks natural explanations of objects and events and therefore sanctions a naturalist philosophy or world-view. One error in that thinking appears when we reflect that scientific or natural explanation leads always to a search for explanation of its explanations, i.e., to an infinite regress that never reaches ultimate explanation. For example, when told that some chromosomal change explains a new form of life, we ask what explains the chromosomal change. When that is offered, we ask what explains *it*. This line of inquiry, hardly avoidable by thinking people, leads nowadays to the "Big Bang" theory of the origin of the universe, which fails to explain the "Big Bang" itself. This should suffice to show that science does not and never will provide the ultimate conceptions or beliefs in whose light, consciously or not, consistently or not, but always, individuals and societies view the world, find their roles in it, and make their most significant decisions. For their world-view, their governing philosophy, whether they know it or not, individuals and societies look elsewhere than to empirically tested science.

But perhaps even more than to its alleged sanction by science naturalism has owed its appeal to the promise of all-around human progress that its devotees have found in it. Where recent naturalism has been more than a cultural inheritance unthinkingly accepted, where it has been ardently embraced and propagated, it has not simply denied the reality of the transcendent source of man's free mind and conscience that believing Jews and Christians have called God. It has not simply pronounced that conception false. It has pronounced transcendental religion a great obstacle to man's development, a stultifier, an active evil. It has held that man, once naturalistically enlightened, will advance to levels not only of knowledge but also of freedom, social harmony, and rationality higher than any so far attained.

Now one has no difficulty in understanding such naturalism's appeal for men of the 18th and 19th centuries. Within at least the family memories of some, optimistic naturalism had proved a useful weapon in winning free of the "divine-right" kings, inquisitorial theologians, and religious wars consequent on the religious corruption of the

Renaissance. One easily understands how naturalism got conceived as humanism; many of its first consequences were humanly benign.

Yet today must we not acknowledge that naturalism has failed to deliver the progress promised by its champions? The hopes it once engendered no longer fire adult imaginations: we know that man is not evolving toward perfection, that in fact man is not significantly evolving; where Marxism has triumphed it has established tyranny, not a realm of freedom; instead of uplifting the instinctive animal in us, Freudianism has licensed him. For over a century naturalism has drawn thought and practice into conformity with itself, at once persuading men that they are essentially brutes yet encouraging them to develop and augment their powers without let or limit—and the results in this century's indices of war, tyranny, fiscal profligacy, suicide, and discontent, and in the dark overhang of nuclear and biological weaponry, look more and more like human regress. Do we not simply pay the evidence its due if we view enthusiasm for the naturalistic doctrines examined in these pages as symptomatic of a singularly bloody century's deep demoralization?

As we seek to regain our balance an obvious truth demands more acknowledgement than has been given it by a generation schooled from early youth to hold in special horror, as history's *summum malum*, the "divine-right" kings, inquisitorial theologians, and religious wars popularly thought to have been medieval and attributed to medieval religion. The obvious truth is that today neither divine-right kings, nor inquisitorial theologians, nor religious wars threaten our humanity. Nor for that matter did they threaten man's humanity for a near millenium in the Middle Ages; like fear of witches they darkened mainly the 16th and 17the centuries.[7] Today our humanity, our being as men, is chiefly threatened by the dictators, revolutionaries, and "useful idiots" whom naturalistic writers and educators have produced. Once that obvious truth has been acknowledged, and once science has been seen not to sanction a world-view of any kind, naturalism may lose much of its appeal. As it does, religion that affirms realities transcending the empirical world may once more attract wide adult attention.

One more of the many chastened shifts from atheism to religious faith that history has recorded seems all the more likely when we reflect that what is sound and convincing in our modern Doctors' thought—Freud's sense of man's persistent irrationality, Marx's perception of the transiency of existing social and economic orders, and Darwin's conviction that descent with modification does somehow occur—harmonizes easily with and in fact was largely anticipated by the religious teaching of a millenium-and-a-half ago. That living creatures have in some way changed hugely over time, that no social or economic order can be permanent, that irrationality remains a persistent human failing—all that was known and dwelt upon by the Doctors of the Church. What religious wisdom never has known and never will assert is the self-cancelling proposition that man is only a creature of circumstance and instinct, that he is locked within a system of natural causes that makes freedom and conscience empty words.

One therefore can envision a generation driven to philosophical reflection by this century's events coming to view transcendental religion as the prophetic mind of Giambattista Vico viewed it. That profound and philosophical historian saw transcendental religion as a force that over the ages emerged again and again to prevent man's final regress into bestiality, a force that providentially preserved men's difference from the beasts.[8]

Conclusion — Notes

1. Loc. cit., pp. 55-57.

2. Letter of May 22, 1860, in *The Life and Letters of Charles Darwin*, Francis Darwin ed., London, 1898, vol. II, p. 105. Freud argued similarly in Lecture XXXV, "The Question of a *Weltanschauung*," in *The Complete Introductory Lectures on Psychoanalysis*, transl. and ed. James Strachey, 1966.

3. Paley, *Natural Theology*, 1860, pp. 317-18 (text of the London 1802 edition).

4. Gould, *Ever Since Darwin*, 1977, p. 39.

5. See Merton's contribution to *Sorokin in Review*, Philip J. Allen ed., 1963, pp. 337, 367.

6. Kaufmann, *Critique of Religion and Philosophy*, 1958, p. 416f.

7. Chartered towns and corporations, knightly orders, universities, all of them self-governing and protected by statute, and above all the Church and its various agencies, narrowly restricted the power of medieval kings. As for the Inquisition, H.C. Lea, *A History of the Inquisition of the Middle Ages*, 1922, observes that during the Middle Ages (5th or 6th century to 14th) the Inquisition was usually inactive, its infrequent penalties "mild." It was only when the study of Roman law revived toward the end of the Middle Ages that the Inquisition began to grow into the horror it later became. Europe's wars of religion began in the 16th century. Most of the ills popularly attributed to the Middle Ages and their religion occurred centuries later, during the late Renaissance. The great curse of the Middle Ages was not tyranny but disease. A skewed conception of the Middle Ages has given naturalism much of its appeal.

8. The New Science of Giambattista Vico, transl. Bergin and Fisch, 1961, pp. 382-83.

INDEX

From the same publisher:

〜〜〜

Classic European Short Stories Robert Beum (ed) 278 pages. Paper: $6.95.
Doctors of Modernity: Darwin, Marx, & Freud by R. F. Baum. Paper: $7.95.
A Better Guide than Reason: Studies in the American Revolution by M. E. Bradford. Intro. by Jeffrey Hart. Paper: $5.95.
Generations of the Faithful Heart: On the Literature of the South by M. E. Bradford. Paper: $6.95.
Dynamics of World History by Christopher Dawson. Edited by John J. Mulloy. 509 pages. Paper: $9.95.
Christianity in East & West by Christopher Dawson. Edited by John J. Mulloy. 224 pages. Paper: $5.95.
Escape from Scepticism: Liberal Education as if Truth Mattered by Christopher Derrick. Paper: $4.95
Joy Without a Cause: Selected Essays by Christopher Derrick. 248 pages. Paper: $5.95.
Angels, Apes, and Men by Stanley L. Jaki. Paper: $5.95.
The Angel and the Machine: The Rational Psychology of Nathaniel Hawthorne by E. Michael Jones. Paper: $10.95.
Edmund Burke: A Genius Reconsidered by Russell Kirk. 225 pages. Paper $8.95.
Eliot and His Age by Russell Kirk. 490 pages. $12.95.
Enemies of the Permanent Things: Observations of Abnormity in Literature and Politics by Russell Kirk. 312 pages. $9.95.
The Intemperate Professor and Other Cultural Splenetics by Russell Kirk. Paper: $7.95.
Why Flannery O'Connor Stayed Home (Vol. I of the trilogy, *The Prophetic Poet & the Spirit of the Age*) by Marion Montgomery. 486 pages. Cloth: $24.95.
Why Poe Drank Liquor (Vol. II of the trilogy, *The Prophetic Poet & the Spirit of the Age*) by Marion Montgomery. 440 pages. Cloth: $24.95.
Why Hawthorne Was Melancholy (Vol. III of the trilogy, *The Prophetic Poet & the Spirit of the Age*) by Marion Montgomery. 585 pages. Cloth: $24.95.
The Impatience of Job by George W. Rutler. Paper: $4.95.
Cosmos & Transcendence: Breaking Through the Barrier of Scientistic Belief by Wolfgang Smith. Paper: $8.95.
Christianity & the Intellectuals by Arther Trace. Paper: $5.95.
Citizen of Rome: Reflections from the Life of a Roman Catholic by Frederick D. Wilhelmsen. 345 pages. Paper: $7.95.

(Please add $1.00 for postage and handling.)